St. Boniface, Manitoba

(Save From The Fire)

1825-1834

Baptisms, Marriages and Burials

Gail Morin

© 2016

Sources:

Photocopies of original records saved from the fire

Ancient Registers of Saint Boniface, 1825-1834, P. Ant. Champagne, o.p.i.c., April-May 1970

Repertoire des Mariages de Saint-Boniface (Manitoba) 1825-1983, Publication #67, (1985), Volume 1, Le Centre de Genealogie S.C., compiled by Julien Hamelin S.C., Printed by Hubert Houle S.C.

Special Assistance: Mary McClammy for obtain the photocopies of the original records from the Portland, Oregon Genealogical Library

Special Assistance: Denis Garand, French translations

Trascription Notes:

When the transcriber entered additional information it is enclosed in [brackets].

The spelling in the entries is the same as the transcription.

The spelling in the headings may have been changed to ease alphabetical sorting.

St.Boniface, Manitoba (Save From The Fire) 1825-1834 Baptisms, Marriages and Burials

..., Angelique
    B-559, Angelique, baptized 31 March 1833, age over 3 years ..., Godmother: Isabelle McGillis, C. E. Poire priest. (page 95-96)

..., Cha...: B-596, Cha ..... baptized 26 May 1833 ... (page 102)

..., Charles
    B-100, Charles (unknown), baptized 14 August 1825, age about one month, born of unknown parents, Godfather: Pierre Falcon, Godmother: Marie Grant, Jn Harper priest. (page 8)

..., Charlotte
    B-411, Charlotte, baptized 1 March 1832, age about 59 years, Godmother: Josephte Fagnant, F. Boucher priest. (page 56)

..., Charlotte
    B-448, Charlotte ..., baptized 17 June 1832, daughter of ... and Louise Duheme. (page 67)

..., Charlotte
    B-602, Charlotte, baptized 26 May 1833, age about 80 years, Godmother: Louise Millet, F. Boucher priest. (page 104)

..., Charlotte
    See Nicholas Ducharme dit Charon

..., Francois
    B-554, Francois ..., baptized 4 March 1833, born 24..., Godfather: Basile Delorme, Godmother: Magdeleine Thomas, F. Boucher priest. (page 94-95)

..., Jacque
    B-602, Jacque, baptized 2 February 1830, born 29 January 1830, the mother known by the name La Fran..., Godfather: Augustin Nolin (signed), Godmother: Margueritte Marchand, Fr. Boucher priest. (page 38)

..., Jean Baptiste
    B-663, Jean Baptiste, baptized 15 September 1833, born 6 June 1833, of unknown parents, Godfather: Jean Baptiste Morin, Godmother: Euphrosine .., J. N. Ev de Juliopolis. (page 108)

..., Josephte
    B-535, Josephte, baptized 5 February 1833, age about 32 years, Godmother: Marguerite, F. Boucher, priest. (page 87)

St.Boniface Register 1825-1834 (Saved From The Fire)

..., Josephte

     See Richard Dagneau and Josephte

..., Josephte

     See Jean Baptiste Dubois and Josephte

..., : M-10, ... in the presence of Benjamin Marchand and Joseph Delauney, Ths. Destroismaisons priest. (page 1)

..., Marguerite

     B-131, Marguerite, wife of Etienne Comtois, baptized 16 October 1825, age 38 years, Godmother: Angelique Cris, J. N. Ev de Juliopolis. (page 16)

..., Marguerite

     B-132, Marguerite, baptized 16 October 1825, born July 1825, parents unknown, Godfather: Augustin Nolin (signed), Godmother: Catherine Macon, J. N. Ev de Juliopolis. (page 16)

..., Marguerite:

     S-37, Marguerite -, buried 22 December 1832, died day before yesterday ... (page 85)

..., Marie Anne: B-590, Marie Anne .., baptized 22 May 1833, age ... (page 101)

..., Marie

     B-492, Marie __, baptized 9 September 1832, age 5 months, daughter of Michel .. and Louise Descoteaux, Godfather: Joseph Parenteau, Godmother: Emilie Brousse, G. A. Belcourt priest. (page 75)

..., Marie: See Pierre Desrochers

..., Susanne

     B-603, Susanne, baptized 7 February 1830, age about 44 years, wife of Joseph La Fournaise, Godmother: Josephte ..., Fr. Boucher priest. (page 38)

..., Suzanne: See Pierre Desrochers

..., unknown: B__, ..., Godfather: Jean Baptiste Morin, Godmother: Julie Ducharme, F. Boucher priest. (page 93)

..., unknown: B__, ... baptized 16 September 1832, .., Godfather: Alexis Cariere, Godmother: Angelique Cariere, F. Boucher priest. (page 75-76)

..., unknown: B-491, __, baptized 9 September 1832, Godmother: Genevieve widow Depes [?], G. A. Belcourt priest. (page 74-75)

..., unknown: B-542, __, baptized 20 February 1833, born yesterday of the legitimate marriage of __ (page 92)

..., unknown: B-722, .. Baptized 26 January 1834 ... (page 126)

..., unknown: B-781, .. baptized 18 May 1834 ... (page 128)

..., unknown: S__, .. buried 9 May 1834, of ... and Josephte .. (page 127)

****[no entries for B-603-630]

***[B-513-531 missing]

***[B-542-545, and S-39 missing or incomplete]

***[B-722-775 is missing]

Adam, Antoine
    B-585, Antoine Adam, baptized - October 1829, born 15 April, of the legitimate marriage of Jean Baptiste Adam, free man, and Magdeleine Lemire, Godfather: Jean Baptiste Larence, Godmother: Louise, wife of Jean Bte. Larence, Jn Harper priest. (page 33)

Adam, Genevieve
    B-471, Genevieve Adam, baptized 3 August 1832, born yesterday daughter of of Joseph Adam and Angelique Racette, Godfather: Antoine Caron, Godmother: Genevieve, widow Dece, G. A. Belcourt priest. (page 71)

Adam, Joseph and Angelique Racette
    M-106, Joseph Adam, adult son of Jean-Baptiste Adam and Josephte Montagnaise, married 22 February 1830, Angelique Racette, adult daughter of Charles Racette and Josephte Sauteuse, in the presence of Charles Racette and Benjamin Marchand, Fr. Boucher priest. (page 43)

Adam, Marie
    B-412, Marie Adam, daughter of Jean Baptiste Adam and Louise Quebec, age about 33 years, Godmother: Genevieve Benoit, widow Dece [Dease], G. A. Belcourt priest. (page 58)

Adam, Marie
    See Guillaume Rocheleau and Marie Adam

Alary, Andre
B-828, Andre Alary, baptized 10 August 1834, son of Michel Alary and a Sa..., Godfather: Andre Carriere, Godmother: .... (page 136)

Alary, Antoine
B-845, Antoine Alary, baptized 24 August 1834, age one year, son of Louis Alary and Marguerite Desjarlais, Godfather: Antoine Gosselin, Godmother: Marie Roy, J. B. Thibault priest. (page 141)

Alary, Catherine
B-843, Catherine Alary, baptized 24 August 1834, age 6 years, daughter of Louis Alary and Marguerite Desjarlais, Godfather: Francois Lyonais, Godmother: Catherine Martineau, J. B. Thibault priest. (page 141)

Alary, Catherine
B-860, Catherine Alary, baptized 21 September 1834, age 3 years, daughter of Antoine Alary and Josephte Caplet, Godfather: J... Rouseau dit Beaumet, Godmother: Marie Caplet, J. B. Thibault priest. (page 146)

Alary, Charlotte
B-844, Charlotte Alary, baptized 24 August 1834, age 3 years, daughter of Louis Alary and Marguerite Desjarlais, Godfather: Joseph Parenteau, Godmother, Charlotte Sauve, J. B. Thibault priest. (page 141)

Alary, Francois
B-842, Francois Alary, baptized 24 August 1834, age 7 years, son of Louis Alary and Marguerite Desjarlais, Godfather: Michel Alary, Godmother: Josephte Miny, J. B. Thibault priest. (page 141)

Alary, Joseph
B-869, Joseph Alary, baptized 28 September 1834, age 6 years, son of Antoine Alary and Angelique Caplet, Godfather: Jean Baptiste Boisvert, Godmother: Monique Hamelin, J. B. Thibault. (page 148)

Alary, Louis
B-868, Louis Alary, baptized 28 September 1834, age 6 years, son of Antoine Alary and Angelique Caplet, Godfather: Isidore Bernier, Godmother: Charlotte, J. B. Thibault priest. (page 148)

Alary, Magdeleine

B-859, Magdeleine Alary, baptized 21 September 1834, age 3 years, daughter of Antoine Alary and Josephte Caplet, Godfather: Vital Turcotte, Godmother: Magdeleine Caplet, J. B. Thibault priest. (page 146)

Alary, Pierre

B-893, Pierre Alary, baptized 23 November 1834, age 2 years, son of Michel Alary and Marie of the nation of Serpents, Godfather: Joseph Berio, Godmother: Francoise St.Germain, J. N. Ev. de Juliopolis. (page 155)

Alary, Pierre

B-870, Pierre Alary, baptized 28 September 1834, age 2 years, son of Antoine Alary and Angelique Caplet, Godfather: Louis Gagnon, Godmother: Magdeleine Caplet, J. B. Thibault priest. (page 148)

Allie, Joseph

B-122, Joseph Allie, baptized 29 September 1825, born today of the legitimate marriage of Joseph Allie, resident of this mission, and Marguerite Dubois, Godfather: Jean Baptiste Morin, Godmother: Ma. Ducharme, Jn Harper priest. (page 14)

Amberland, Henriette

B-111, Henriette Amberland, without condition baptized 24 September 1825, age about 17 years, daughter of George Amberly and Suzanne Perrot from the canton of Berne Switzerland, Ths. Destroismaisons. (page 11)

Amelin, Elisabeth

B-547, Elisabeth Amelin, baptized 28 February 1833, born today of the legitimate marriage of Jacques Amelin and Marie Hamel, Godfather: Joseph Deganne, Godmother: Elisabeth, G. A. Belcourt priest. (page 93)

Amelin, Francois Xavier

B-397, Francois Xavier Amelin, baptized 14 February 1832, born yesterday, of the legitimate marriage of Joseph Amelin and Therese Ducharme, Godfather: Leon Amelin, Godmother: Isabelle Amelin, F. Boucher priest. (page 51)

Amelin, Francoise

B-445, Francoise Amelin, baptized 10 June 1832, born 28 December 1831, of Jean Baptiste Amelin and Francoise Ducharme, Godfather: Louis Amelin, Godmother: Francois Beleau, G. A. Belcourt priest. (page 67)

St.Boniface Register 1825-1834 (Saved From The Fire)

Amelin, Louis

B-629, Louis Amelin, baptized 12 April 1830, born 5 September 1828, of the legitimate marriage of Jacques Amelin and Marie Hamel, Godfather: Jean-Baptiste Devis, Godmother: Victoire W...., Fr. Boucher priest. (page 46)

Amelin, Monique

B-410, Monique Amelin, baptized 4 March 1832, born today, of the legitimate marriage of Leon Amelin and Isabelle Vendal, Godfather: Antoine Vendal, Godmother: Marguerite, F. Boucher priest. (page 56)

Arcand, Joseph and Marie Gesson

M-59, Joseph Arcand, adult son of Alexis Arcand and Genevieve Picher, the father and mother of the parish of Cap-Sante in Canada, married 29 February 1832, Marie Gesson, daughter of Francois Gesson dit Vestreau and Louise Decoste, in the presence of Jean Baptiste Gariepy and Michel Klyne, G. A. Belcourt priest. (page 54)

Arcand, Joseph

B-555, Joseph Arcand, baptized 4 March 1833, born yesterday, of the legitimate marriage of Joseph Arcand and Marie Vestrau, Godfather: Francois Morin, Godmother: Marie Gladu, F. Boucher priest. (page 95)

Assiniboine, Joseph

B-823, Joseph Assiniboine, baptized 31 July 1834, age 3 years, son of Assiniboine, Godfather: L. Bousquet (signed), Godmother: Angelique, J. B. Thibault priest. (page 136)

Assiniboine, Marie

B-822, Marie Assiniboine, baptized 31 July 1834, age 5 years, daughter of Assiniiboine, Godfather: Pierre Carron, Godmother: Marguerite, J. B. Thibault priest. (page 135)

Azur, Arsene

B-684, Arsene Azur, baptized 3 November 1833, born yesterday of the legitimate marriage of Antoine Azur and Charlotte, Godfather: Antoine Laroque, Godmother: Therese Sauteuse, C. E. Poire priest. (page 113)

Azur, Joseph

S-26, Joseph Azur, buried 31 January 1832, died suddenly day before yesterday, age 71 years, in the presence of Francois Lionais and Antoine Azur his son, J. N. Ev. de Juliopolis priest. (page 51)

Baudoin, Antoine

B-558, Antoine Baudoin, baptized 31 March 1833, born 28 March 1833, of the legitimate marriage of Joseph Baudoin and Marie (Montagnaise), Godfather: Antoine Pilon, Godmother:

Francoise (Montagnaise), C. E. Poire priest. (page 95)

Beauchamp, Charles
B-806, Charles Beauchams, baptized 10 July 1834, age 4 years, son of Charles Beauchams and Catherine Falardeau, Godfather: Andre Carriere, Godmother: Angelique Dion, J. B. Thibault priest. (page 132)

Beauchamp, Francoise
B-121, Francoise Beauchamp, baptized 25 September 1825, age 17 years daughter of Jean Baptiste Beauchamp & Josephte Daze, Godmother: Genevieve Larence, Ths. Destroismaisons priest. (page 12)

Beauchamp, Francoise
See Francois Courchene and Francoise Beauchamp

Beauchamp, Jerome
B-662, Jerome Beauchamp, baptized 15 September 1833, born yesterday, of the legitimate marriage of Pierre Beauchamp and Marie Comtois, Godfather: Jerome Beauchamp, Godmother: Josephte Delorme. (page 108)

Beauchamp, Marguerite
B-807, Marguerite Beauchams, baptized 10 July 1834, age one year, daughter of Charles Beauchams and Catherine Falardeau, Godfather: P[aul] Boucher, Godmother: Josephte Dion, J. B. Thibault priest. (page 132)

Beauchemin, Marie Anne Millet dit
See Louis Contois dit Morin and Marie Anne Millet dit Beauchemin

Beauchemin, Marie
B-550, Marie Beauchemin, baptized 6 March 1833, born yesterday of the legitimate marriage of Benjamin Beauchemin and Marie Parenteau, Godfather: Antoine Azure, Godmother: Charlotte Peltier, the father was absent. G. A. Belcourt priest. (page 94)

Beaudouin, Alexis
B-601, Alexis Beaudouin, baptized 31 January 1830, born in the night, of the legitimate marriage of Joseph Baudouin, free man, and Marie Le Roux, Godfather: Antoine __, Godmother: Angelique Plante, Frs. Boucher. (page 38)

Beaupre, Dion-Donne
B-502, Dion-Donne Beaupre, baptized 3 December 1832, born day before yesterday of the legitimate marriage of Joseph Beaupre and Louise Cadotte, Godfather: Joseph Ritchot, Godmother: Marguerite Dubois, G. A. Belcourt priest. (page 83)

Beaupre, Jacques

B-623, Jacques Beaupre, baptized 28 March 1830, born yesterday of the legitimate marriage of Joseph Beaupre, barrel maker, and Susanne Cadot, Godfather: Jacques Cardinal, Godmother: Louise Godon, F. Boucher priest. (page 45)

Beaupre, Joseph and Susanne Cadot

M-29, Joseph Beaupre, barrel maker of this mission, adult son of the late Pierre Beaupriest and the deceased Marie Anne Martin, the father and mother lived in the Parish of Sorel, District of Montreal, married 8 November 1825, Susanne Cadot, adult daughter of Augustin Cadot, farmer, and a Sauteuse of Leech Lake, in the presence of Francois Labranche friend of the husband, and Augustin Cadot father of the wife, Ths. Destroismaisons priest. (page 19)

Belanger, Francoise

B-77, Francoise Belanger, baptized 3 July 1825, age about 35 years, daughter of Andre Belanger and a Montagnaise, Godfather: Francois Dore, Godmother: Anna Henriette Taitt, Ths. Destroismaison priest. (page 4)

Belanger, Francoise:

See Michel Normand and Francoise Belanger

Belanger, Louise

B-443, Louise Belanger, baptized 10 June 1832, age 15 years, daughter of Louis Belanger and Josephte, Godmother: Angelique Tourangeau, G. A. Belcourt priest. (page 67)

Belanger, Louise

See Joseph Pelle dit Lafleur and Louise Belanger

Belhumeur, Jean Monet dit

B-480, Jean Monet dit Belhumeur, baptized 23 September 1832, born 15 September 1832, of the legitimate marriage of Andre Monet dit Belhumeur and Marguerite Maron, Godfather: Joseph Pageai, Godmother: Magdelaine Falcond, G. A. Belcourt priest. (page 77)

Bellenger, Bazile and Magdeleine Pied noirs

M-57, Bazile Bellenger, adult son of the late Louis Bellenger and the deceased Marie Label, the father and mother of the parish of St.Vincent de Paul, married 25 January 1832, Magdeleine of the nation of pieds noirs, widow of the deceased Den.... (page 50)

Belley, Josephte

See Amable Fafard dit Delorme and Josephte Belley

Belly, Josephte

B-500, Josephte Belly, baptized 25 November 1832, age 33 years, daughter of Antoine Belly and a Crise, Godmother: Angelique Dion, J. N. Ev. de Juliopolis. (page 82)

Berard, Denys

B-801, Denys Berard, baptized 8 July 1834, age 6 years, son of Louis Berard and Catherine Hughes, Godfather: Pierre Berard, Godmother: Genevieve Begnet, J. B. Thibault priest. (page 131)

Berard, Elizabeth

S-46, Elizabeth Berard, buried 28 June 1829, died yesterday, over six years old, daughter of Pierre Berard and Marie Fortin, in the presence of Jean Baptiste Latourelle and Jacques Goulet, J. N. Ev. de Juliopolis priest. (page 26)

Berard, Eustache

B-802, Eustache Berard, baptized 8 July 1834, age 5 years, son of Louis Berard and Catherine Hughes, Godfather: Isidore Bernier (signed), Godmother: Angelique Nolin, J. B. Thibault priest. (page 131)

Berard, Isabelle

B-803, Isabelle Berard, baptized 8 July 1834, age 3 years, daughter of Louis Berard and Catherine Hughes, Godfather: Olivier Ducharme, Godmother: Marguerite Dease, J. B. Thibault priest. (page 131)

Berard, Louis and Catherine Hughes

M-136, Louis Berard, adult son of Pierre Berard and Elisabeth Vignalat, of the District of Montreal, married 6 October 1834, Catherine Hughes, adult daughter of James Hughes and a Corbeau, in the presence of Antoine Carron and Pierre Berard, J. B. Thibault. (page 150)

Berard, Louis

B-800, Louis Berard, baptized 8 July 1834, age 7 years, son of Louis Berard and Catherine Hughes, Godfather: Alexandre Ducharme (signed A. Ducharme), Godmother: Marie Anne Dease, J. B. Thibault priest. (page 131)

Berard, Marguerite

B-634, Marguerite Berard, baptized 6 August 1833, born yesterday, of the legitimate marriage of Pierre Berard and Marie Fortin, Godmother: Marguerite Dease, C. E. Poire priest. (page 105)

Berard, Marie

[B-804], [Marie Berard, baptized 8 July 1834], age about 2 months, daughter of Louis Berard and Catherine Hughes, Godfather: Alexandre Ducharme (signed A. Ducharme), Godmother: Marie Fortin, J. B. Thibault priest. (page 131-132)

Berard, unknown
     B-573, ..., baptized [6 April 1833], .., of Pierre Berard and a Sauteuse, Godfather: Louis Le Blanc, G. A. Belcourt priest. (page 98)

Bercier, Alexis
     B-698, Alexis Barcier, baptized 8 November 1833, born yesterday, of the legitimate marriage of Jean Baptiste Barcier and Marie St.Pierre, Godfather: Charles Ducharme, Godmother: Marguerite Barcier, G. A. Belcourt priest. (page 117)

Berio, Joseph and Isabelle Duval
     M-111, Joseph Berio, adult son of the deceased Joseph Berio and the deceased Marie Anne Gauthier, of Trois Rivieres, married 7 October 1833, Isabelle Duval, minor daughter of the late .. Duval and Francoise ..., in the presence of Francois Charon and Jean Baptiste Perrault, J. N. Ev. de Juliopolis. (page 110)

Berland, Alexandre Duboishue dit
     B-417, Alexandre Duboishue dit Berland, baptized 18 March 1832, born yesterday of the legitimate marriage of Alexandre Duboishue dit Berland and Emillie Wells, Godfather: Cuthbert Grant, Esquire, Godmother: Josephte Grant, F. Boucher priest. (page 59)

Berland, Marie Duboishue
     B-607, Marie Duboishue Berland, born and baptized 7 February 1830, of the legitimate marriage of Alexandre Duboishue Berland and Emilie Wils, Godfather: A.... Monet, Godmother: Magdeleine Falcon, Jn. Harper priest. (page 40)

Berland, Pierre Dubois hue dit
     S-51, Pierre Dubois hue dit Berland, buried 2 November 1829, d. night before last, age about 69 years, in the presence of Andre Carriere and Thomas Pivin, Fr. Boucher priest. (page 33)

Bleau, Suzanne
     B-103, Suzanne Bleau, baptized 19 August 1825 born today, of the legitimate marriage of Antoine Bleau and Marguerite Bourdon, Godfather: Alexis Crochiere, Godmother: Suzanne Ducharme (signed), Jn Harper priest. (page 9)

Boisvert, Jean Baptiste and Susanne Bourret
     M-135, Jean Baptiste Boisvert, adult son of Francois Boisvert and Catherine Bellegarde, the father and mother of the Riviere du Loup District of Trois-Rivieres, married 23 September 1834, Susanne Bourret, adult daughter of the late Joseph Bourret and Susanne Muru [Munro], in the presence of Joseph Caplet and Charles Bellegarde, J. B. Thibault priest. (page 147)

Boisvert, Louis and Marguerite Sauteuse

   M-122, Louis Boisvert, adult son of the deceased Louis Boisvert and the late Marie Courval of Terrebonne, married 20 January 1834, Marguerite Sauteuse, in the presence of Jean Yanche and Louise Carriere, J. B. Thibault priest. (page 125)

Bonami, Magdeleine

   B-566, Magdeleine Bonami, baptized 22 July 1829, born yesterday, of the legitimate marriage of Alexis Bonami and Marguerite Grenon, Godfather: Jean Yanche, Godmother: Marie McGillis, wife of Cuthbert Grant, J. N. Ev. de Juliopolis priest. (page 29)

Bonneau, Joseph

   B-428, Joseph Bonneau, baptized 6 May 1832, age 5 months, son of Antoine Bonneau and Angelique Delorme, of White Horse prairie, Godfather: Francois Delorme, Godmother: Suzanne Bonneau, G. A. Belcourt priest. (page 61)

Bonneau, Marguerite

   S-34, Marguerite Bonneau, buried 1 October 1832, age 13 months, daughter of [Pierre] Bonneau and Louise Gariepi of White Horse Plains, in the presence of Lo... Gariepi and Charles Montigny, G. A. Belcourt priest. (page 78)

Bonneau, Norbert

   B-560, Norbert Bonneau, baptized 25 March 1833, born yesterday of the legitimate marriage of Antoine Bonneau and Angelique Delorme, Godfather: Norbert Delorme, Godmother: Francoise, Frs. Boucher priest. (page 96)

Bonneau, Pierre and Louise Guarriepy

   M-99, Pierre Boneau, adult son of Jean Baptiste Boneau and the deceased Louise Indian, married 1 February 1830, Louise Guarriepy, minor daughter of Louis Guarriepy, blacksmith, and the deceased Josephte Sauteuse, in the presence of Louis Garriepy, Jean Bap. Boneau, Joseph Guilbeau, Jn Harper priest. (page 40)

Bonneau, Pierre

   B-598, Pierre Bonneau, baptized 26 May 1833, age 2 months, son of Pierre Bonneau and Louise Gariepy, Godfather: Pierre Boyer, Godmother: Josephte Ducharme, C. E. Poire priest. (page 103)

Bonneau, Susanne

   See Eusebe Ledoux and Susanne Bonneau

St.Boniface Register 1825-1834 (Saved From The Fire)

Botineau, Joseph and Angelique Cardinal
M-78, Joseph Botineau, adult son of the late Charles Botineau and Marguerite Sauteuse, married 17 September 1832, Angelique Cardinal, minor daughter of Jacques Cardinal and Josephte Assiniboine, in the presence of Jacques Cardinal and Basile Belanger, F. Boucher priest. (page 76)

Boucher, Francois
B-592, Francois Boucher, baptized 25 May 1833, age 18 years, son of Francois Boucher .., Godfather: Joseph Desmarais... (page 102)

Boucher, Jean Baptiste and Julie de Rocheblave
M-22, Jean Baptiste Boucher, carpenter, adult son of P. Boucher and Angelique Olivier, of Riviere du Loup District of Trois-Rivieres, married 26 September 1825, Julie de Rocheblave, minor daughter of Pierre de Rocheblave Esquire and Marguerite Boucher, in the presence of Benjamin Marchand and Francois Dore, Ths. Destroismaisons priest. (page 12 - 13)

Boucher, Jean Baptiste
S-47, Jean Baptiste Boucher, miller, buried 16 July 1829, d. 14 July 1829, age about 33 years, in the presence of Francois Bruneau (signed), Benjamin Lagemoniere (signed), Jn. Harper priest. (page 27)

Boucher, Louise
See Jean Baptiste Charbonneau and Louise Boucher

Boucher, Paul and Francoise St.Germain
M-64, Paul Boucher, adult son of the deceased Etienne Boucher and Marie Sioux, married 5 March 1832, Francoise St.Germain, adult daughter of the late Pierre St.Germain and Louise, in the presence of Je.... and Jean Baptiste Ho... (page 56)

Boucher, Reine
See Charles Racette and Reine Boucher

Bouke, Andrew
B-488, Andrew Burck [Bourke], baptized 2 September 1832, born 10 April 1832, of John Burck [Bourke] and Nancy Campbell, Godfather: Jean Baptiste Latourelle, Godmother: Arc... Marsolet, G. A. Belcourt priest. (page 74)

Bourke, Anne
B-557, Anne Bourke, baptized 28 June 1829, born __ May of the year previous, of the legitimate marriage of John Palmer Bourke and __ Campbell, Godfather: Jean Baptiste Lagimoniere, Godmother: Angelique Nolin, J. N. Ev. de Juliopolis priest. (page 26)

Bourke, Zoe

    B-659, Zoe Bouk, baptized 21 August 1833 at Rainy Lake, born 11 January 1833, of Charles William Bouk and Isabelle Dore, Godfather: Augustin Roussille, Frs. Boucher priest. (page 107)

Bourret, Susanne

    See Jean Baptiste Boisvert and Susanne Bourret

Bouvet, Francois and Marguerite Marchand

    M-113, Francois Bouvet, adult son of Francois Bouvet and the deceased Marie Perreault, the father and mother from Montreal, married 4 November 1833, Marguerite Marchand, minor daughter of Benjamin Marchand and Marguerite Nadeau, in the presence of Pierre Leblanc (signed) and Benjamin Marchand, C. E. Poire priest. (page 113-114)

Bouvet, Francois

    B-863, Francois Bouvet, baptized 23 September 1834, born this morning of the legitimate marriage of Francois Bouvet and Marguerite Marchand, Godfather: Louis Galarneau, Godmother: Julie Marchand, J. B. Thibault priest. (page 147)

Boyer, Helene

    B-713, Helene Boyer, baptized 4 January 1834, born yesterday of the legitimate marriage of Jean Baptiste Boyer and Helene McMillan, Godfather: Joseph Pager, Godmother: Marie Letendre, J. B. Thibault priest. (page 123)

Boyer, Jean Baptiste and Helene McMillan

    M-95, Jean Baptiste Boyer, adult son of Pierre Boyer and Josephte Led... of Vaudreuil, married 5 February 1833, Helene McMillan, adult daughter of James McMillan and Marie Letendre, in the presence of Louis Letendre and Jacques Cardinal, Francois Boucher priest. (page 88)

Braban, Augustin

    B-677, Augustin Braban, baptized 20 October 1833, age 5 years and 7 months, of Augustin Braban and a Montagnais, Godfather: Alex. ..., J. B. Thibault priest. (page 111)

Braban, Charlotte

    B-780, Charlotte Braban, baptized 18 May 1834, age 12 years, daughter of Augustin Braban and a Montagnaise, Godmother: Genevieve Grant, .. (page 128)

Braban, Genevieve

    B-779, Genevieve Braban, baptized 18 May 1834, age 13 years, daughter of Augustin Braban and a Montagnaise, Godmother: Charlotte Sauvez, J. B. Thibault priest. (page 128)

Bramner, Nancy
        B-484, Nancy Bramner, baptized 12 August 1832, born 29 July last, of Alexandre Bramner and Betsey Twat, Godfather: Francois Delorme, Godmother: Marie McGillis, G. A. Belcourt priest. (page 73)

Branconier, Adeline
        B-490, Adeline Branconier, baptized 7 September 1832, born yesterday, of the legitimate marriage of Jean Baptiste Branconier and L(ouise) Beauchemin, Godfather: Benjamin Beauchemin, Godmother: Marie Parenteau, G. A. Belcourt priest. (page 74)

Branconier, Amable and Francoise Picher
        M-118, Amable Branconier, adult son of Am[able] Branconier and Genevieve Lafrieniere, of the Berthier District of Montreal, married [between 25 and 26] November 1833, Francoise Picher, adult daughter of Louis Picher and the deceased Josephte Montagnaise, in the presence of Paul Bo[ucher] and Antoine Caron, G. A. Belcourt priest. (page 120)

Branconnier, Reine
        B-715, Reine Branconnier, baptized 12 January 1834, born today, daughter of Amable Branconnier and Francoise Piche, Godmother: Francoise ..., C. E. Poire priest. (page 124)

Brazeau, Marguerite
        B-793, Marguerite Brazeau, baptized 2 June 1834, born this morning of the legitimate marriage of Louis Brazeau and Louise Lagane, Godfather: Antoine Villebrun, Godmother: Archange Marsolet, J. N. Ev de Juliopolis. (page 129)

Brickler, Marie-Anne
        B-110, Marie-Anne Brickler, baptized 23 September 1825, born yesterday of the the legitmate marriage of Antoine Brickler (signed Zundan Brickler), of this mission and Elizabeth Rendichbaker, Godfather: Michel Renier, Godmother: Sophie Fournier (signed Sophie Adele), Ths. Destroismaisons priest. (page 11)

Briere, Jean Baptiste and Francoise Serpent
        M-101, Jean Baptiste Briere, farmer, adult son of the late Louis Briere and the deceased Marie Lapointe of the parish of Terrebone, District of Montreal, married 8 February 1830, Francoise of the Nation of Serpens, in the presence of Henri Poitras and Joseph Fagnan, Jn Harper priest. (page 41)

Brousse, Pierre Elie
        B-433, Pierre Elie Brousse, baptized 16 May 1832, born yesterday, of the legitimate marriage of Charles Gaspard Brousse and Marguerite Lanoue, Godfather: Francois Bruneau (signed), and Genevieve, widow of Dece, G. A. Belcourt priest. (page 64)

Bruce, Jean Baptiste

S__, Jean Baptiste Bruce, buried 27 May 1833, age 7 years, son of Gaspard Bruce and Marguerite Lanoue, in the presence of Pierre B... and Charles Larance, F. Boucher priest. (page 104)

Bruce, Pierre

B-589, Joseph Bruce, baptized [between 17-22 May] 1833, born today of the legitimate marriage of Pierre Bruce and Marguerite Bonneau, Godfather: Joseph Guilbeau, Godmother: Marguerite, F. Boucher priest. (page 101)

Bruiere, Jean-Baptiste

S-52, Jean-Baptiste, buried 21 November 1829, died in the night, son of Cecile Bruiere and an unknown father, in the presence of Antoine Caron and Pierre __, Frs. Boucher priest. (page 34-35)

Brunoche, Francoise

S-54, Francoise Brunoche, died 11 February 1830, buried 15 February 1830, wife of Jean Baptiste Morand, age 30 years, in the presence of Charles Racette and Benjamin Marchand, Frs. Boucher priest. (page 42)

Bruyere, Marguerite

B-425, Marguerite Bruyere, baptized 22 April 1832, age 17 years, born before the legitimate marriage of Jean Baptiste Brueyere and a Serpente, Godmother: Marie George, G. A. Belcourt priest., F. Boucher priest. (page 61)

Bruyere, Marie

See Pierre Poitras and Marie Bruyere

Cadot, Marie

B-702, Marie Cadot, baptized 18 November 1833, age 28 years, daughter of [Laurent] Cadot and Susanne Mackegone, Godmother: Angelique Nolin, G. A. Belcourt priest. (page 118)

Cadot, Susanne

See Joseph Beaupre and Susanne Cadot

Cadot,Marie

See Jean Baptiste St.Cyr and Marie Cadot

Cadotte, Louise

B-402, Louise Cadotte, baptized 24 February 1832, born 2 February 1832, of Benjamin Cadotte and a Sauteuse, Godfather: Joseph Turpin, Godmother: Louise Versaille, F. Boucher priest. (page 52)

Cadotte, Marie
> See Joseph Brissard dit St.Germain and Marie Cadotte

Cadotte, Pierre and Jean Baptiste
> B-660-661, baptized 11 September 1833, Pierre Cadotte, age 3 years, Jean Baptiste, age one year, sons of Laurent Cadotte and Isabelle Machkegone, Godfather: Pierre St.Germain, Godmother: Josephte Charron dit __, J. N. ev. de Juliopolis. (page 107)

Campbell, Marguerite
> B-685, Marguerite Campbell, baptized 23 August 1833 at Lac la Croix, born 8 January 1833, daughter of Colin Campbell and Elizabeth McGilvray, Godfather: Frs. Boucher priest (signed), Frs. Boucher priest. (page 114)

Caplet, Joseph and Angelique Guiboche
> M-101, Joseph Caplet, adult son of the late Joseph Caplet and the deceased Josephte Pinel, married 18 February 1833, [Angelique] Guiboche, adult daughter of the late Louis Guiboche, in the presence of Jean Baptiste Versail and Jean Baptiste Saint-Cyr, F. Boucher priest. (page 91-92)

Caplet, Magdeleine
> B-591, Magdeleine Caplet, baptized 25 May 1833, age 15 years, daughter of Joseph Caplet and Angelique Guiboche, Godmother: Marie Crebassa, F. Boucher priest. (page 102)

Caplet, Marie
> B-590, Marie Caplet, baptized 25 May 1833, age 16 years, daughter of Joseph Caplet and Angelique Guiboche, Godmother: Francoise St.Germain, F. Boucher priest. (page 102)

Cardinal, Angelique
> See Joseph Botineau and Angelique Cardinal

Cardinal, Genevieve
> B-120, Genevieve Cardinal, baptized 25 September 1825, age 13 years on last August, daughter of Toussaint Cardinal and a Montagnaise, Godmother: Josephte Laroque, Ths. Destroismaisons priest. (page 12)

Cardinal, Genevieve
> B-580, Genevieve Cardinal, baptized 15 April 1833, born today of the legitimate marriage of Jean Baptiste Cardinal and Josephte Ducharme, Godfather: Andre Millet, Godmother: Susanne Ducharme, F. Boucher priest. (page 99)

Cardinal, Theophile
    S-73, Theophile Cardinal, buried 8 September 1834, died this night, age two months, son of [Jeremie] Cardinal and Louise Adam, in the presence of Pierre Carron and Isidore Be[rnier], J. B. Thibault priest. (page 144)

Cardinal, Theophine
    B-821, Theophile Cardinal, baptized 30 July 1834, born yesterday, of the legitimate marriage of Jeremie Cardinal and Louise Adam, Godfather: Francois Courchaine, Godmother: Angelique Racette, J. B. Thibault priest. (page 135)

Caron, Angelique
    See Louis Laferte and Angelique Caron

Caron, Antoine
    S__, Antoine Carron, buried 19 July 1834, died in an accidental drowning in the Assiniboine River 15 July 1834, age 17 years, son of Antoine Carron and Angelique St.Germain, in the presence of Jean Baptiste Lagimoniere and Alexis Goulet, J. N. Ev de Juliopolis. (page 135)

Caron, Marguerite
    B-711, Marguerite Caron, baptized 1 January 1834, born yesterday, of the legitimate marriage of [Antoine Caron] and Angelique St.Germain ... (page 122)

Caron, Marie-Anne
    B-622, Marie-Anne Caron, born and baptized 18 March 1830, of the legitimate marriage of Antoine Caron, farmer, and Angelique Saint-Germain, Godfather: Andre Carriere [different writing] , Godmother: Marie Anne Rivard, Fr. Boucher priest. (page 44-45)

Carrier, Angelique
    See Benjamin Lagimoniere and Angelique

Carriere, Andre and Marie Anne Rivard
    M-104, Andre Cariere, adult son of Andre Cariere and Angelique Dion, of this mission, married 22 February 1830 Marie Anne Rivard, minor daughter of Jean Baptiste Rivard and Therese Bellenger, her father and mother, in the presence of Benjamin Marchand and Charles Racette, Fr. Boucher priest. (page 43)

Carriere, Andre and Angelique Dion
    M-24, Andre Carriere, resident of this mission, adult son of Joseph Carriere and Marguerite St.Sauveur, of Boucherville, District of Montreal, married Angelique Dion, adult daughter of the late Thomas Dion and a Cree, in the presence of Joseph Delaunay and Benjamin Marchand, Ths. Destroismaisons priest. (page 13 - 14)

Carriere, Andre, Louis and Louise

B-113, 114, 115, baptized 25 September 1825, Andre, age 18 on 28 July, Louis, age 10 years on 14 February, Louise, age 12 years on 20 Februray, children of Andre Carriere, of St.Boniface, and Angelique Dion, Godfather of the boys Pierre Versailles, Godmother of the girls Marguerite Brien, Ths. Destroismaisons. (page 11)

Carriere, Catherine

B-511, Catherine Carriere, baptized 26 December 1832, born today of the legitimate marriage of Alexis Carriere and Susanne Ducharme, Godfather: Andre Carriere, Godmother: Catherine, F. Boucher priest. (page 86)

Carriere, Charles Toussaint

B-683, Charles Toussaint Carriere, baptized 3 November 1833, born yesterday of the legitimate marriage of Andre Carriere and Marie Anne Rivard, Godfather: Louis Carriere, Godmother: Angelique Carron, C. E. Poire priest. (page 113)

Carriere, Genevieve

B-141, Genevieve Carriere, baptized 10 November 1825, born yesterday of the legitimate marriage of Andre Carriere, resident of this mission and Angelique Dion, Godfather: Jean Baptiste Letendre, Godmother: Anne Henriette Taitte [Anna Henriette Tait], Jn Harper priest. (page 19)

Carriere, Louis and Julie Marchand

M-124, Louis Carriere, of Andre Carriere and An[gelique Lyon], married 21 January 1834, Julie Marchand, minor daughter of Benjamin Marchand and Marguerite Nadeau, Present the fathers of the bride and groom, Andre Carriere and Benjamin Marchand, J. N. de Juliopolis. (page 125-126)

Chalifoux, Isabelle

See Louis Landry and Isabelle Chalifoux

Chalifoux, Louise

B-562, Louise Chalifoux, baptized 4 April 1833, age 16 years, of Michel Chalifoux and Isabelle Collin, Godfather: Joseph Arcand, Godmother: Magdeleine Ross, G. A. Belcourt priest. (page 96)

Chalifoux, Michel

S__, Michel Chalifoux, ancient voyageur, buried 26 October 1833 at St.Francois Xavier, White Horse Plains, died 25 October 1833 at the same place, age 70 years, in the presence of Joseph Gilbeau and Louis Gariepy, G. A. Belcourt priest. (page 113)

Champagne, Pierre

     B-586, Pierre Champagne, baptized 17 May 1833, born yesterday of the legitimate marriage of Emmanuel Champagne and Marguerite Laroque, Godfather: Antoine Laroque, Godmother: Marguerite Nadeau, C. E. Poire priest. (page 101)

Charbonneau, Adelaide

     B-864, Adelaide Charbonneau, baptized 26 September 1834, born this morning of the legitimate marriage of Jean Baptiste Charbonneau and Louise Boucher, Godfather: Amable Naud, Godmother: Marie, wife of Francois Lambert, J. N. Ev de Juliopolis. (page 147)

Charbonneau, Jean Baptiste and Louise Boucher

     M-117, Jean Baptiste Charbonneau, son of ..., married 25 November 1833, [Louise Boucher], ..., G. A. Belcourt priest. (page 119-120)

Charron, Antoine

     B-585, Antoine Charron, baptized 16 May 1833, born of the legitimate marriage of Nicolas Charron and Charlotte Abinoch, Godfather: Alexandre Charron, Godmother: Magdelaine Grouet, C. E. Poire. (page 100-101)

Charron, Dominique and Sophie Heneau

     M-116, Dominique Charon, adult son of Francois Charon and __ Rivet, married 25 November 1833, Sophie Heneau, minor daughter of Charles Heneau and Marie Grey, in the presence of Jean Baptiste Perreault and Jean Baptiste Dumoulin, J. N. Ev de Juliopolis. (page 119)

Chartrand, Isabelle

     B-460, Isabelle Chartrand, baptized 15 July 1832, age 5 years, daughter of Joseph Chartrand and a Sauteuse, Godfather: Francois St.Germain, Godmother: Isabelle McGillis, G. A. Belcourt priest. (page 70)

Chatelain, Louis

     B__, Louis Chatelain, baptized 21 August 1833 at Rainy Laky, age 1 month and 8 days, son of Nicolas Chatelain and (Anne) Cartier, Godfather: Frs. Boucher (signed), Frs. Boucher priest. (page 107)

Choret, Augustin

     B-483, Augustin Choret, baptized 14 October 1832, born day before yesterday of the legitimate marriage of Prosper Choret and Magdelaine Cardinal, Godfather: Augustin Brisebois, Godmother: Marie Anne Beauchemin, J. N. Ev de Juliopolis. (page 78)

St.Boniface Register 1825-1834 (Saved From The Fire)

Cloutier, George

B-853, Geo[rge Cloutier], baptized 6 September 1834, [son of Jean Baptiste Cloutier] and Josepthe Racette, Godfather: Pierre ..., Godmother: Marguerite Marchand, J. B. Thibault priest. (page 143-144)

Cloutier, Joseph

B-618, Joseph Cloutier, baptized 26 February 1830, born 23 February 1830, of the legitimate marriage of Francois Cloutier and Catherine Holmes, Godfather: Francois ...., Godmother: Marie Larocque, Jn. Harper priest. (page 44)

Cloutier, Marguerite

S-76, Marguerite Cloutier, buried 6 October 1834, died 3 October 1834, age .., daughter of Jean Baptiste Cloutier and .., in the presence of Isidore Bernier and Pierre Carron, J. B. Thibault priest. (page 150-151)

Colin, Amable and Jean Baptiste

B-691, 692, baptized 1 September 1833, Amable Collin, born 5 December 1832, son of Michel Collin and a Indian woman, Jean Baptiste Collin, born 13 October 1832, of Antoine Collin and a Sauteuse, Godfather of the two infants: Pierre Morin, Godmother: Josephte Hamel, Frs. Boucher priest. (page 115)

Collin, Isabelle

B-406, Isabelle Collin, baptized 28 February 1832, age 46, daughter of Antoine Collin and Louise, Godmother: Marguerite Labine, F. Boucher priest. (page 53)

Collin, Isabelle

See Michel Richard and Isabelle Collin

Collin, Louise

B-144, Louise Collin, baptized 20 November 1825, age 17 years, daughter of Joseph Collin and Josephte Sauteuse, Godmother: Josephte Lo.., Ths Destroismaisons priest. (page 20)

Collin, Louise

See Louis Villebrun and Louise Collin

Collin, Rosalie

See Francois Desmarais and Rosalie Collin

Collin, Susanne

B-142, Susanne Collin, baptized 14 November 1825, born 25 October 1825, of the legitimate marriage of Jean Baptiste Collin, free man of this mission, and Elisabeth Henry, Godfather: Jean Baptiste Lepine, Godmother: Suzanne Lorin, Ths. Destroismaisons priest. (page

20

20)

Comtois, Etienne and Marguerite Sarcie

M-26, Etienne Comtois, son of the deceased Comtois and the deceased St.Georges, of the parish of [St.Michel d'Yamaska crossed out] [on the bottom + Lanoraie] married 17 October 1825 Marguerite Sarcie, in the presence of Thimothee Dionne, Victor Chenier, J. N. Ev de Juliopolis. (page 17)

Comtois, Marie, Louis and Jean Baptiste

B-133, 134, 135, Marie, Louis, and Jean Baptiste Comtois, baptized 16 October 1825, Marie, age 14? years, Louis, age 12 years, Jean Baptiste, age 9 years, children of Etienne Comtois and Marguerite Sarcie, Godmother: Marie: Helene Cameron, Godfather: Louis: Leon Chenier, Godfather: Jean Baptiste: Dominique Charon, J. N. Ev de Juliopolis. (page 16)

Contre, Angelique

B-712, Angelique Contre, baptized 2 January 1834, age 22 years, daughter of the deceased Jean Baptiste Contre and Louise Montagnaise, Godmother: Genevieve, wife of Prosper Chorette, J. B. Thibault priest. (page 123)

Cornic, Julie

B-489, Julie Cornic, baptized 21 October 1832, born .., of the legitimate marriage of Jean Baptiste Cornic and Julie Charon, Godfather: Jean Yanche, Godmother: Josephte Severight, J. N. Ev de Juliopolis. (page 80)

Coulombe, Joseph

B-152, Joseph Coulombe, baptized 18 December 1825, Winnipeg River, age 6 months and 8 days, son of Francois Coulombe, Engage of the Company and a Mandan, Godfather: Joseph Dagneau, Godmother: Genevieve Cameron, Ths. Destroismaisons priest. (page 22)

Courchene, Francois and Francoise Beauchamp

M-28, Francois Courchene, free man of this mission, adult son of Jean Baptiste Courchene and the deceased Josephte Delaunay, the father and mother of the parish of Baie du Febvre, District of Trois-Rivieres married 8 November 1825, Francoise Beauchamp, minor daughter of Jean Baptiste Beauchamp and Josephte Daze, the father and mother of this mission, in the presence of Amable Naud and Louis Larrivee friends of the groom and Paul Daze and Joseph Allie friends of the bride, Ths Destroismaisons priest. (page 18-19)

Courchene, Francois

B-832, Francois [Courchene], baptized 14 August 1834, born of the legitimate marriage of F[rancois Courchene and Francoise Beauchamp], Godfather: Pierre Beauchamp, Godmother: Josephte Belley, C. E. Poire priest. (page 137-138)

Courchene, Marguerite
       B-489, Marguerite Courchene, baptized 3 September 1832, born today of the legitimate marriage of Francois Courchene and Francoise Beauchamp, Godfather: (Louis) Letendre, Godmother: Josephte Daze, G. A. Belcourt priest. (page 74)

Crebassa, Marie
       See Louis Galarneau and Marie Crebassa

Cris, Marguerite
       See Edouard Herman and Marguerite Cris

Cris, Marie Anne
       B-126, Marie Anne, baptized 9 Octobert 1825, age 70 years, of the nation of Cris, Godmother: Josephte Grant, Ths. Destroismaisons priest. (page 14)

Cris, Marie
       See Jean McDonald and Marie Cris

Cyr, Anonyme
       S-52, Anonyme Cyr, buried 10 January 1843, born 26 December 1833, died day before yesterday of the legitimate marriage of Louis Cyr and Catherine Delormier [?], in the presence of Joseph Vandal and Toussaint Vaudry, C. E. Poire omi. (page 124)

Cyr, Jean Baptiste
       B-855, Jean Baptiste Cyr, baptized 14 September 1834, age about 10 years, son of Louis Cyr and Louise Gosselin, Godfather: .. Ducharme, Godmother: Angelique Nolin, J. B. Thibault priest. (page 144)

Cyr, Joseph
       B-474, Joseph Cyr, baptized 12 August 1832, born 23 July 1832, of the legitimate marriage of Louis Cyr and Catherine Lormiere, Godfather: Joseph Vandal, Godmother: Josephte Lacheorotiere, J. N. Ev. de Juliopolis priest. (page 71)

Cyr, Magdeleine
       B-534, Magdeleine Cyr, baptized 30 January 1833, born yesterday of the legitimate marriage of Francois Cyr and Victoire Vivier, Godfather: Olivier Roc-Brune, Godmother: Magdeleine Piche, F. Boucher priest. (page 87)

Cyr, Magdeleine dit Assiniboine
       S-38, Magdeleine Cyr dit Assiniboine, buried 11 February 1833, age 11 days, daughter of Francois Cyr and Victoire Vivier, in the presence of Antoine Lafreniere and Charles ..., G. A. Belcourt priest. (page 88)

Dagneais, Pierre

B-104, Pierre Dagenais, baptized 5 September 1825, age __ the 25 December last, son of Antoine Dagenais, free man, and Louise Assiniboine, Godfather: Pierre Ducharme, Godmother: Josephte Marleau, Ths. Destroismaisons priest. (page 10)

Dagneau, Joseph

B-150, Joseph Dagneau, baptized 18 December 1825, Winnipeg River, born 22 October 1825, of the legtimate marriage of Joseph Dagneau, Engage of the Company, and Genevieve Cameron, Godfather: John McDonald, Esquire, Godmother: Marie Potras, his wife, Ths. Destroismaisons priest. (page 22)

Dagneau, Marie

B-716, Marie Dagneau, baptized 17 January 1834, born of the legitimate marriage of Richard Dagneau and Josephte, Godfather: Jean Baptiste Mar..., Godmother: Susanne Dagneau, J. N. Ev de Juliopolis. (page 124)

Dagneau, Richard and Josephte

M-93, Richard Dagneau, adult son of the late Richard Dagneau and the deceased Josephte Fortier of Boucherville, married 5 February 1833, Josephte, in the presence of Joseph Parenteau and Andre Carriere, F. Boucher priest. (page 87)

Daniel, Jean Baptiste

B-548, Jean Baptiste Daniel, baptized 4 March 1833, born 27 February 1833, of unknown parents, Godfather: Joseph Parenteau, Godmother: Marie Letendre, J. N. Ev. de Juliopolis. (page 93)

Danis, Marguerite

B-538, Marguerite Danis, baptized 17 February 1833, age 28 years, Godmother: Josephte, C. E. Poire priest. (page 90)

Danis, Marguerite

See Louis Lamirande and Marguerite Danis

Dauphine, Charlotte

See Louis Picher and Charlotte Dauphine

Davely, John

S-__, John Davelly, buried 9 March 1832, age 5 months, daughter of Lawrence Davelly and Britgitfe Conniff, in the presence of Paschal Montour and Peter Heder... G. A. Belcourt priest. (page 59)

Davis, Jean Baptiste
B-668, Jean Baptiste Davis, baptized 25 September 1833, born yesterday of the legitimate marriage of Jean Baptiste Davis and Josephte Sauteuse, Godfather: Jean Baptiste Louiseau, Godmother: Marguerite, J. B. Thibault priest. (page 109)

Davis, Josephte
B-563, Josephte Davis, baptized 19 July 1829, w/o condition, age about one year, legitimate daughter of Jean Baptiste Davis and Josephte Sauteux, Godfather: Jean Baptiste Marcelet, Godmother: Josephte Severet, Jn. Harper priest. (page 28)

de la montage de Roche, Marie
See Pierre Desrochers and Marie de la montage de Roche

Decoste, Louise
B-404, Louise Decoste, baptized 28 February 1832, daughter of Francois Decoste and a Indian of the Masquegone tribe, age 30 years, Godmother: Marguerite, F. Boucher priest. (page 53)

Decoste, Louise
See Ambroise Le Clair dit Alard and Louise Decoste

Deganne, Infant
S-36, Infant Deganne, buried 18 December 1832, born, christened, died day before yesterday, infant of Joseph Deganne and Elisabeth Hamelin, in the presence of Paschal Montour and Pierre Carron, G. A. Belcourt priest. (page 85)

Deganne, Joseph and Elisabeth Hamelin
M-65, Joseph Deganne, adult son of Jean Baptiste Deganne and Louise Huneau, m. 5 March 1832, Elisabeth Hamelin, minor daughter of Jacques Hamelin and Angelique Tourengeau, in the presence of Louis Marsolet and Louis Boucher, G. A. Belcourt priest. (page 57)

Deganne, Marguerite
B-708, Marguerite Deganne, baptized 6 December 1833, born this morning of the legitimate marriage of Joseph Deganne and Isabelle Hamelin, Godfather: Louis Hamelin, Godmother: Marguerite Sansregret, J. N. Ev de Juliopolis. (page 122)

Deganne, Marguerite
S-66, Marguerite Deganne, buried 20 August 1834, age 7 months, died yesterday, daughter of Joseph Deganne and Isabelle Hamelin, in the presence of Louis Hamelin and Joseph Hamelin, C. E. Poire priest. (page 139)

Delaunay, Francois

S-53, Francois Delaunay, buried 25 November 1829, died 23 November 1829, age about 16 years, son of Francois Delaunay and Louise Sauteuse, in the presence of Joseph Parenteau and Francois Delaunay, Frs. Boucher priest. (page 35)

Delaunay, Marguerite

See Jean Baptiste Letendre and Marguerite Delaunay

Delorme, Alexis

B-590, Alexis Delorme, baptized 15 November 1829, born 30 October 1829, of the legitimate marriage of Joseph Delorme and Brigitte Villebrun, Godfather: Alexis Bonami, Godmother: Therese Villebrun, Frs. Boucher priest. (page 34)

Delorme, Amable Fafard dit and Josephte Belley

M-80, Amable Fafard dit Delorme, adult son of the deceased Joseph Fafard dit Delorme and the deceased Charlotte Brissette, of the parish of Berthier in Canada, married 26 November 1832, Josephte Belley, adult daughter of the deceased Antoine Belley and a Crise, in the presence of Andre Carriere and Paschal [Montour]. (page 82)

Delorme, Catherine Eneau dit

B-81, Catherine Eneau dit Delorme, baptized 17 July 1825, daughter of the legitimate marriage of Joseph Eneau dit Delorme and Brigitte, Godfather: Pierre Parenteau, Godmother: .. Delore, Jn Harper priest. (page 6)

Delorme, Francois and Angelique Malaterre

M-76, Francois Delorme, free man of this mission, widower of Marguerite Demarais, married 25 June 1832 Angelique Malaterre, minor daughter of Jean Baptiste Malaterre and Angelique Adam, in the presence of Louis Blondeau and Basile Plante, F. Boucher priest. (page 69)

Delorme, Louis

B-503, Louis Delorme, baptized 8 December 1832, born this night of the legitimate marriage of Joseph Delorme and Brigitte Villebrun, Godfather: Louis Villebrun, Godmother: Louise Collin, J. N. Ev. de Juliopolis. (page 83)

Delorme, Magdelaine

B-138, Magdelaine Delorme, baptized 23 October 1825, born 13 September 1825, of Francois Delorme and Angelique Metote, Godfather: Jean Baptiste Rocbrune, Godmother: Magdelaine wife of Ferdinand, Jn Harper. (page 17)

Demers, Pierre and Josephte Sauteuse
M-138, Pierre Demers [Dumais], adult son of the deceased Pierre Demers and the deceased Marguerite Laprade, the father and mother from Berthier, District of Montreal, married 4 November 1834, Josephte Sauteuse, in the presence of Joseph Dagneault and Sieur William Shaw (signed), J. B. Thibault priest. (page 153)

Deschamps, August and Josephte
B-105 and 106, baptized 5 September 1825, Anne, age 5 years on the last day of August and Josephte Deschamps, age - 18 May last, daughter of Jean Baptiste Deschamps, free man, and Josephte Amel, Godfather: Antoine Caron, Godmother: Angelique St.Germain, Ths. Destroismaisons priest. (page 10)

Deschamps, Jean Baptiste
B-140, Jean Baptiste Deschamps, baptized and born 4 November 1825, of Jean Baptiste Deschamps and Josephte Hamel, Godfather: Pierre Ducharme, Godmother: Catherine wife of Pierre Ducharme, Jn Harper priest. (page 18)

Deschamps, Joseph
B-687, Joseph Deschamps, baptized 1 September 1833 at Fort William, born 1 May 1833, son of Joseph Deschamps and Josephte Hamel, Godfather: Martin Lami dit Desfonds, Godmother: .., Frs. Boucher priest. (page 114)

Deschamps, Marguerite
B-415, Marguerite Deschamps, baptized 9 March 1832, age about 3 years, daughter of Pierre Deschamps and a Sauteuse, Godfather: Alexandre Ducharme, Godmother: Louise, F. Boucher priest. (page 59)

Descoteaux, Joseph and Marie Vivier
M-55, Joseph Descoteaux, adult son of Joseph Descoteaux and Magdeleine Lafreniere, married 17 January 1832, Marie Vivier, adult daughter of Francois Vivier and Josephte Montagnaise, in the presence of Francois Vivier, father of the bride, and Charles Racette, friend of the groom, J. N. Ev de Juliopolis priest. (page 48)

Descoteaux, Joseph and Charlotte Lanoue
M-72, Joseph Descoteaux, of this mission, married 15 May 1832, Charlotte Lanoue, adult daughter of the late Joseph Lanoue and a Sauteuse, in the presence of Joseph Yanche and Jean Baptiste Frederic, G. A. Belcourt priest. (page 64)

Descoteaux, Joseph and Marie-Anne Lafournaise
M-105, Joseph Decoteau, adult son of Joseph Decoteau and Louise Deschamps married 22 February 1830, Marie-Anne Lafournaise, minor daughter of Joseph Lafournaise and a Cree, in the presence of Joseph Lafournaise and Joseph Decouteau, Fr. Boucher priest. (page 43)

Descoteaux, Joseph

B-495, Joseph Descoteau, baptized 10 November 1832, born yesterday of the legitimate marriage of Joseph Descoteau and Marie Vivier, Godfather: Joseph Descoteau, Godmother: Josephte, F. Boucher priest. (page 81)

Descoteaux, Joseph

B-614, Joseph Decoteau, baptized 21 February 1830, age about 22 yers, son of Joseph Decoteau and Louise Deschamps, Godfather: Jean Baptiste Latourelle, Fr. Boucher priest. (page 42)

Descoteaux, Joseph

B-386, Joseph Descoteaux, baptized 16 January 1832, age 23 years, son of Joseph Descoteaux and Magdeleine Lafreniere, Godfather: Jean Baptiste Letendre, J. N. Ev de Juliopolis priest (page 47)

Descoteaux, Joseph

S__, Joseph Descoteaux, buried 8 August 1833, died today, age 84 years, in the presence of Antoine Le Gros and Gilbert Berio, C. E. Poire priest. (page 105)

Descoteaux, Marguerite

B-880, Marguerite Descoteaux, baptized 19 October 1834, born yesterday of Joseph Descoteaux and Marie Vivier, Godfather: Olivier Paul, Godmother: Louise Andre, J. B. Thibault priest. (p. 151)

Desfont, Marguerite

B-92, Marguerite Desfont, baptized 4 August 1825, age about 5 years, "demi" daughter of Joseph Desfont, free man, of St.Boniface, and Josephte Desbiens, Godfather: Charles Gaspard Brousse, Godmother: Magdelaine Boucher, Ths. Destroismaisons priest. (page 7)

Desjarlais, Francois and Louise

B- 79 and B-80, Francois and Louise Desjarlais, baptized 13 July 1825, Francois, age 5 years on 2 January last, Louise, age one on 12 November last, children of Antoine Desjarlais, free man, and Suzanne Alari, Godparents for Francois: Benjamin Marchand and Marie Harrison, Godparents for Louise: Louis Lapierre and Isabella Normand, Ths. Destroismaisons priest. (page 5)

Desjarlais, Francois

B-490, Francois Desjarlais, baptized 30 September 1832, born today of the marriage of Francois Desjarlais and - Sauteuse, Godfather: Jean Baptiste Wilki, Godmother: Francoise St.Germain, F. Boucher priest. (page 80)

Desjarlais, Isabelle
    B-856, Isabelle Desjarlais, baptized 14 September 1834, age 4 years, daughter of Antoine Desjarlais and Catherine Alary, Godfather: Thomas Harrison, Godmother: Marguerite Marchand, J. B. Thibault priest. (page 145)

Desjarlais, Jean Baptiste
    B-857, Jean Baptiste Desjarlais, baptized 14 September 1834, age 2 years, daughter of Antoine Desjarlais and Catherine Alary, Godfather: Alexis Goulet, Godmother: Julie Marchand, J. B. Thibault priest. (page 145)

Desjarlais, Thomas
    B-826, Thomas Desjarlais, baptized 10 August 1834, age 2 years, bon of an unknown father and Judith Desjarlais, Godfather: Thomas Harrison, Godmother: Marie Caplet, C. E. Poire priest. (page 136)

Deslauriers, Antoine Legault dit and Genevieve Lacourse
    M-137, Antoine Legault dit Deslauriers, son of [Antoine] Legault dit Des Lauriers and the deceased Louise Beaulieu, the father and mother of St.Benoit, District of Montreal, married 28 October 1834, Genevieve Lacourse, widow of Bazile Plante, in the presence of Louis Galarneau and Jean Baptiste Collin, J. B. Thibault priest. (page 152-153)

Desmarais, Francois and Marguerite Villebrun
    M-94, Francois Desmarais, widower of Rosalie Collin, married 5 February 1833, Marguerite Villebrun, adult daughter of the late Louis Villebrun and Marie-Anne Collet, in the presence of Louis Villebrun and Andre Carriere, F. Boucher priest. (page 87-88)

Desmarais, Francois and Rosalie Collin
    M-17, Francois Desmarais, adult son of Jean Baptiste Desmarais and Josephte Sauteuse, married 27 June 1825, Rosalie Collin, adult daughter of Antoine Collin and Josephte Paul, in the presence of Joseph Allie and Francois .., Ths. Destroismaisons priest. (page 4)

Desmarais, Francois
    B-__, Francois Desmarais, baptized 26 June 1825, age twenty, on August eighteenth last, son of Jean Baptiste Desmarais and Josephte Sauteuse, Godfather: Charles Gaspard Brousse, Godmother: Marguerite Lanoue, Ths Destroismaisons priest. (page 3)

Desmarais, Francois
    B-709, Francois Desmarais, baptized 15 December 1833, born yesterday of the legitimate marriage of Francois Desmarais and Marguerite Villebrun dite Plouf, Godfather: Joseph Pelle dit Laf..., Godmother: Therese Villebrun dite Plouf, G. A. Belcourt priest. (page 122)

St.Boniface Register 1825-1834 (Saved From The Fire)

Desmarais, Michel and Marguerite Vivier
M-96, Michel Desmarais, free man, minor son of Jean Baptiste Desmarais and Louise of the nation of Sauteuse, married 11 January 1830 Marguerite Vivier minor daughter of Alexandre Vivier and Marie Anne of the nation of Assiniboine, Present Alexis Vivier, father of the bride, and Joseph Guilbeau, Jn Harper priest. (page 37)

Desmarais, Michel
B-598, Michel Desmarais, baptized 10 January 1830, age 19 years, son of Jean Baptiste Desmarais and Louise Sauteuse, Godfather: Louis Guarriepy, Jn. Harper priest. (page 37)

Desmarais, Severe
B-125, Severe Desmarais, baptized 9 October 1825, born 24 May, legitimate son of Joseph Desmarais and .. Amelin, Godfather: Pierre Ducharme, Godmother: Catherine, Jn. Harper. (page 14)

Desrochers, Pierre and Marie de la montage de Roche
M-102, Pierre Desrochers, adult son of the late Pierre Desrochers and Charlott of the nation of Cris married 8 February 1830, Marie de la montagne de Roche [of the Rocky Mountains], in the presence of Joseph Fagnan and Donald McGillis, Jn Harper priest. (page 41)

Desrochers, Pierre
B-608 through B-611, Pierre Desrochers, age about 40 years, Godfather: Joseph Fagnan, and Marie, age 42 years, Godmother: Marguerite Lavigne, Suzanne, age 50 years, Godmother: Marguerite Morin, and Francoise, age 40 years, Godmother: Marguerite Poitras, parents sauvages, baptized 7 February 1830, Jn Harper priest. (page 40)

Dion, Angelique
B-116, Angelique Dion, age 38 years, baptized 25 September 1825, daughter of Thomas Dion and a Cris, Godmother: Anne Henriette Tritt [Tait], Ths. Destroismaisons. (page 11)

Dion, Angelique
See Andre Carriere and Angelique Dion

Dion, Marguerite
B-430, Marguerite Dion, baptized 8 May 1832, daughter of Joseph Dion and a Cree, age about 46 years, Godmother: Catherine, F. Boucher priest. (page 62)

Dion, Marguerite
See Jean Baptiste Martel and Marguerite Dion

St.Boniface Register 1825-1834 (Saved From The Fire)

Dubois, Francois and Angelique Lariviere

M-__, Francois Dubois, of St.Boniface, adult son of Francois Dubois and Josephte Frappier of St.Cuthbert, married 26 July 1825, Angelique Lariviere, adult daughter of of the deceased Charles Lariviere and a Cris, in the presence of Charles Tranchemontagne and Antoine Lise, Ths. Destroimaisons priest. (page 7)

Dubois, Jean Baptiste and Josephte

M-112, Jean Baptiste Dubois, adult son of the late Amable Dubois and the deceased Francoise Baudouin, the father and mother from Terrebonne district, married 29 October 1833, Josephte, widow of Joseph .., in the presence of Jean Baptiste Dupuis and Jean Baptiste ... (page 112-113)

Dubois, Joseph

S-32, Joseph Dubois, buried 29 May 1832, died day before yesterday, age about 60 years, in the presence of Joseph Hupe and A. Canisne [?], F. Boucher priest. (page 74)

Dubois, Marguerite

See Joseph Savoyard and Marguerite Dubois

Dubois, Marie

B-419, Marie Dubois, baptized 1 April 1832, born yesterday, of Marie Dubois, father unknown, Godfather: Jean Baptiste Dubois, Godmother: Amable Azure, F. Boucher priest. (page 60)

Dubois, Marie

B-628, Marie Dubois, baptized 5 April 1830, age about 1.. (dix ..), of [Francois] Dubois, cultivator, and Angelique Lariviere, [Godmother]: wife of Antoine Azure, Frs. Boucher priest. (page 46)

Dubois, Susanne

B-588, Susanne Dubois, baptized 2 November 1829, age about 23 years, daughter of Francois Dubois and Angelique Lariviere, Godmother: Marie Harisson, F. Boucher priest. (page 33)

Dubois, Suzanne: See Francois Plourde and Suzanne Dubois

Ducep, Pierre

B-676, Pierre Ducep, baptized 20 October 1833, born 12 October 1833, of the legitimate marriage of Michel Ducep and Emelie Parateau, Godfather: Joseph Parateau, Godmother: Louise Parateau, J. B. Thibault priest. (page 111)

St.Boniface Register 1825-1834 (Saved From The Fire)

Ducharme, Josephte
      B-102, Josephte Ducharme, baptized 14 August 1825, age about 19 years, daughter of Antoine Ducharme and Josephte Villeburn, Godfather: Cuthbert Grant, Godmother: Marie McGillis, Jn Harper priest. (page 9)

Ducharme, Josephte
      See Louis Gariepy and Josephte Ducharme

Ducharme, Nicolas dit Charon and Charlotte
      M-56, Nicolas Ducharme dit Charon, son of Charles Ducharme of the parish of Berthier, married 19 February 1832, Charlotte. (page 49)

Dumas, Charles
      B-874, Charles Dumat [Dumas], baptized 29 September 1834, age one year, son of Michel Dumat and Josephte Contree, Godfather: Augustin Breban, Godmother: Angelique Contree, J. B. Thibault priest. (page 149)

Dumas, Marguerite
      B-873, Marguerite Dumat [Dumas], baptized 29 September 1834, age 4 years, daughter of Michel Dumat and Josephte Contree, Godmother: Angelique Contree, J. B. Thibault priest. (page 149)

Dumas, Michel
      B-872, Michel Dumat [Dumas], baptized 29 September 1834, age 6 years, son of Michel Dumat and Josephte Contree, Godfather: Francois Marillon, Godmother: Charlotte, J. B. Thibault priest. (page 149)

Dumond, Jean
      B-635, Jean Dumond, baptized 17 August 1833, of Jean Dumond and Marguerite Laframboise, Godfather: Gilbert Berio, Godmother: Susanne [Blondeau ?], C. E. Poire priest. (page 106)

Dumoulin, Angelique dit Cornic
      B-858, Angelique Dumoulin dit Cornic, baptized 21 September 1834, born this morning of the legitimate marriage of Jean Baptiste Dumoulin dit Cornic and Julie Charon, Godfather: Francois Charon, Godmother: Susanne Blondeau, J. N. Ev de Juliopolis. (page 146)

Durant, Genevieve
      See Jacques St.Denys and Genevieve Durant

Duval, Isabelle
      See Joseph Berio and Isabelle Duval

Emmery, Nancy
> B-605, Nancy Emmery, baptized 7 February 1830, age about 14 years, daughter of W. Emmery and Agathe Letendre, Godmother: Marie Letendre, Fr. Boucher priest. (page 39)

Eno, Francois
> B-825, Francois Eno, baptized 7 August 1834, born yesterday of Charles Eno and Marie Gray, Godfather: Dominique Ducharme, Godmother: Sophie Eno, J. B. Thibault priest. (page 136)

Fafard, Joseph
> B-569, Joseph Fafard, baptized 6 April 1833, age 18 years, son of Joseph Belley (Fafard) and Josephte Belley, Godfather: Joseph Ritchot, G. A. Belcourt priest. (page 97)

Fafard, Josephte
> B-594, Josephte Fafard, baptized 25 May 1833, .., of Joseph Fafard and Josephte, Godmother: Angelique Nolin .. (page 102)

Fafard, Rosalie
> B-595, Rosalie Fafard, baptized 25 May 1833, .., daughter of Joseph Fafard ..., Godmother: Louise Bellanger ... (page 102)

Fagnant, Antoine
> B-83, Antoine Fagnan, baptized 24 July 1825, born 1 June 1825, of the legitimate marriage of Antoine Fagnan, free man, and Josephte Pelletier, Godfather: Pierre Pelletier, Godmother: Charlotte Pelletier, Jn Harper priest. (page 6)

Fagnant, Catherine
> B-571, Catherine Fagnan, baptized 23 August 1829, born 2 July 1829, of the legitimate marriage of Jean Baptiste Fagnan and Josephte [Monet] dit Belhumeur, Godfather: Joseph Page, Godmother: Marguerite Morin, Jn. Harper priest. (page 30)

Fagnant, Francois and Magdeleine Lemire
> M-82, Francois Fagnand, widower of Charlotte Falardeau, married 27 November 1832, Magdeleine Lemire, widow of Jean Baptiste Adam, in the presence of Louis Gardepy and Jean Baptiste Fagnand, F. Boucher priest. (page 84)

Fagnant, Josephte
> B-101, Josephte Fagnan, baptized 14 August 1825, born 10 August 1825, of the legitimate marriage of Jean Baptiste Fagnan, free man, and Josephte Monet, Godfather: Cuthbert Grant, Godmother: Magdeleine Morin, Jn Harper priest. (page 8)

32

Fagnant, Paul

B-665, Paul Fagnant, baptized 15 September 1833, born 11 September 1833, of the legitimate marriage of Francois Fagnant and Madeleine Lemyre, Godfather: Francois Fagnant [?], Godmother: Marguerite Grant, C. E. Poire priest. (page 108)

Faille, Sophie

B-890, Sophie Faille, baptized 14 November 1834, born this night of the legitimate marriage of Toussaint Faille and Angelique, Godfather: Augustin Brabant, Godmother: Genevieve Grant, J. N. Ev de Juliopolis. (page 154)

Falcon, Catherine

B-599, Catherine Falcon, baptized 26 May 1833, born 21 May 1833, of the legitimate marriage of Pierre Falcon and Marie Grant, Godfather: Cuthbert Grant (signed), Godmother: Marie McGillis, C. E. Poire priest. (page 103)

Falcond, Magdelaine Divertissant dit

See Francois Xavier Gesson and Magdelaine Divertissant dit Falcond

Faris, Marie

See Archibald McIntosh

Fay, Guillaume, Angelique and Magdelaine

B-678, 679, 680, baptized 20 October 1833, Guillaume Fay, age one year [?], Angelique Fay, age 2 years, and 3 months [?], and Magdelaine Fay, age 3 years and 3 months, children of Toussaint Fay and Angelique Contree, Godfather of the two first: J.. Rocheleau, Godmother: Marie Adam, Godfather of the last: Joseph M..., Godmother: Magdelaine Caplet, J. B. Thibault priest. (page 112)

Fenler, Antoine

B-458, Antoine Fenler, baptized 8 July 1832, age one, son of George Fenler and Nancy Black of White Horse Plains, Godfather: Antoine Lafreniere, Godmother: Julie Rocheblave, G. A. Belcourt priest. (page 70)

Fisher, Alexandre

B-861, Alexandre Fisher, baptized 21 September 1834, age 13 years, son of Henry Fisher and Marguerite Lafram[boise], Godfather: Maximilien Genton dit Dauphine, Godmother: Emilie Wenzel, J. B. Thibault priest. (page 146)

Fisher, Bethsy

B-862, Bethsy Fisher, baptized 21 September 1834, age 10 years, daughter of Henry Fisher and Marguerite Laframboise, ... (page 146)

Fleury, Marie

      B-78, Marie Fleury, baptized 6 July 1825, age about 3 months, legitimate daughter of Louis Fleury, engage for the Hudson Bay Company, and Josephte Sauvage, Godfather: Francois Dore, Godmother: Anna Henriette Taitt, Ths Destroismaisons priest. (page 5)

Fontaine, Nancy

      See Archibald McIntosh

Fournier, Francois

      B-630, Francois Fournier, baptized 21 March 1830, born today of Francois Fournier and Angelique Methote, Godfather: Donald McGillis, Godmother: Julie de Rocheblave, Jn Harper priest. (page 46)

Fournier, Julie

      B-438, Julie Fournier, baptized 29 May 1832, born today, of the legitimate marriage of Francois Fournier and Angelique Methote, Godfather: Francois Gesson, Godmother: Magdeleine Divertissant, F. Boucher priest. (page 66)

Gagnon, Francois

      B-491, Francois Gagnon, baptized 28 October 1832, born in the evening of the legitimate marriage of Francois Gagnon and Angelique Marcelet, Godfather: Abraham Martin, Godmother: Isabelle David, F. Boucher priest. (page 80)

Gagnon, Joseph

      B-593, Joseph Gagnon, baptized 25 May 1833, .., son of Joseph Gagnon ..., Godfather: Louis Galarneau.... (page 102)

Galarneau, Louis and Marie Crebassa

      M-98, Louis Galarneau, adult son of Joseph Galarneau and Marguerite Archambault of Repentigny, married 12 February 1833, Marie Crebassa, in the presence of Antoine Dupuis and Andre Gaudry, F. Boucher priest.. (page 89-90)

Gariepy, Jean Baptiste

      B-459, Jean Baptiste Gariepi, baptized 8 July 1832, born yesterday, son of Louis Gariepi and Josephte Ducharme, of White Horse Plains, Godfather: Jean Baptiste Gariepi, Godmother: Marguerite McGillis, G. A. Belcourt priest. (page 70)

Gariepy, Jean Baptiste and Marguerite Sauteuse

      M-63, Jean Baptiste Gariepy, adult son of A. Gariepy and Marguerite Brouillet of the parish of Repentigny, married 29 February 1832, Marguerite of the Sauteuse tribe, in the presence of Jean Baptiste Paul and Joseph Arcand, G. A. Belcourt priest. (page 55-56)

Gariepy, Louis and Josephte Ducharme
> M-21, Louis Gariepy, adult son of Bonaventure Gariepy and the deceased Marie Reine Lalonde of La Chenay, married 15 August 1825, Josephte Ducharme, minor daughter of Antoine Ducharme of Berthier District of Montreal and the deceased Josephte Villebrun, in the presence of Angus McGillis and Pierre Falcon, Jn Harper priest. (page 9)

Gariepy, Louise
> See Pierre Boneau and Louise Guarriepy

Gariepy, Marguerite
> B-575, Marguerite Gariepy, baptized 6 April 1833, age 18 years, daughter of Francois Gariepy and Josephte Hamel, Godmother: Josephte Severight, G. A. Belcourt priest. (page 98)

Gaudry, Marguerite
> B-570, Marguerite Gaudry, baptized 15 August 1829, born yesterday, legitimate daughter of Andre Gaudry and Magdeleine David, Godfather: Thomas Harrison, Godmother: Marguerite Harrison, Jn Harper priest. (page 29)

Gaudry, Marie Magdeleine
> S-72, Marie Magdeleine Gaudry, buried 28 August 1834, died today, age 8 months, daughter of Andre Gaudry and Marie Magdeleine David, in the presence of Pierre Berard and Andre Millet, C. E. Poire priest. (page 143)

Gaudy, Catherine
> See Etienne Lambert and Catherine Gaudy

Genton, Joseph
> B-624, Joseph Genton, baptized 28 March 1830, born today of the legitimate marriage of Maximilien Genton, farmer, and Louise Jerome, Godfather: Jean Baptiste Lepine, Godmother: Victoire Walet, F. Boucher priest. (page 45)

Genton, [Marguerite probably]
> B-456, ..., baptized July 1832, .. of .... and Louise Jerome, Godfather: Andre Carriere, Godmother: Julie Henry, G. A. Belcourt priest. (page 69-70)

Genton, Marie dit Daupine
> See Antoine Rocbrune and Marie Genton dit Daupine

Genton, Maximilien and Marie-Louise Jerome
> M-88, Maximilien Genton, resident of this mission, son of the late Jean Baptiste Genton and the deceased Marie-Louise Lafontaine of Lanoraie, married 15 June 1829, Marie-Louise Jerome, adult daughter of the late Martin Jerome and an Indian, in the presence of Michel Dauphine

and Martin Jerome, Jn. Harper priest. (page 24-25)

Geoge, Suzanne

     B-391, Suzanne George, baptized 15 January 1832, born 31 December 1831, before the legitimate marriage of Pierre George and Marguerite, Godfather: Timothe Dion, Godmother: Josephte, F. Boucher priest. (page 49)

George, Pierre and Marguerite Sauteuse

     M-97, Pierre George, adult son of George and a Serpente, married 12 February 1833, Marguerite Sauteuse, in the presence of Antoine Dupuis and Jean Baptiste Larence, F. Boucher priest. (page 89)

Gervais, Jean Baptiste

     B-720, Jean Baptiste Gervais, baptized 22 January 1834, born yesterday of the legitimate marriage of Benjamin Gervais and Genevieve Larence, Godfather: Jean Baptiste Larence, Godmother: Louise Montagnaise, Jean Bap. Thibault priest. (page 126)

Gervais, Paul

     B-506, Paul Gervais, baptized 27 November 1832, born yesterday of the legitimate marriage of Jean Baptiste Gervais and Magdeleine Bonneau, Godfather: Louis Bonneau, Godmother: Marguerite Boutineau, F. Boucher priest. (page 83)

Gervais, Severe

     B-580, Severe Gervais, baptized 14 October 1829, born 11 October 1829, of the legitimate marriage of Benjamin Gervais, farmer, and Genevieve Lacourse, Godfather: Andre Gaudry, Godmother: Josephte Lagimoniere, Fr. Boucher priest. (page 32)

Gesson, Francois Xavier and Magdelaine Divertissant dit Falcond

     M-73, Francois Xavier Gesson, of White Horse Plains, minor son of Francois Gesson and Louise Lecoste, married 21 May 1832, Magdelaine Divertissant dit Falcond, minor daughter of Pierre Divertissant dit Falcond and Marie Grant, in the presence of Jean Baptiste Alarie and Pierre Divertissant, G. A. Belcourt priest. (page 64-65)

Gesson, Marie

     See Joseph Arcand and Marie Gesson

Gilbert, Louis

     B-418, Louis Gilbert, baptized 27 March 1832, born yesterday, of Etienne Gilbert and Marie Collin. (page 59)

Gladu, Antoine

     B-384, Antoine Gladu, baptized 12 January 1832, age 18 years, son of Charles Gladu and

Marguerite Ross, Godfather: Joseph Arcand, Godmother: Josephte Mandale, G. A. Belcourt, priest. (page 47)

Gladu, Charles and Magdeleine Poitras
    M-81, Charles Gladu, adult son of Charles Gladu and Marguerite Ross, married [27] November 1832, Magdeleine Potras, minor daughter of Andre Potras and Marguerite Grant, in the presence of Charles Gladu and Joseph Guilbaut, F. Boucher priest. (page 83-84)

Gladu, Charlotte
    B-505, Charlotte Gladu, baptized 27 November 1832, age 26 years, daughter of Charles Gladu and Marguerite Ross, Godmother: Francoise Lorin, F. Boucher priest. (page 83)

Gladu, Charlotte
    See James Short and Charlotte Gladu

Gladu, Genevieve
    B-561, Genevieve Gladu, baptized 4 April 1833, age 16 years, daughter of Charles Gladu and Magdelaine Ross, Godmother: Magdeleine Vivier, G. A. Belcourt priest. (page 96)

Godin, Angelique
    B-408, Angelique Godin, baptized 28 February 1832, age 26 years, daughter of Francois Godin and Susanne, Godmother: Josephte Fagnand, F. Boucher priest. (page 54)

Godin, Angelique
    See Jean Baptiste Paul and Angelique Godin

Godon, Josephte
    B-108, Josephte Godon, baptized 11 September 1825, age about six years, daughter of Louis Godon and Louise Assiniboine, Godfather: Benjamin Marchand, Godmother: Josephte Marleau, Jn Harper priest. (page 10)

Gonneville, Antoine
    B-454, Antoine Gonneville, baptized 1 July 1832, born yesterday of the legitimate marriage of Antoine Gonneville and Marguerite Labine of White Horse Plains, Godfather: Francois Paul, Godmother: Josephte Esclave, G. A. Belcourt pre. (page 69)

Gosselin, Michel
    B-597, Michel Gosselin, baptized 6 June 1833, age 2 weeks, of Antoine Gosselin and Marie Roi, Godfather: Joseph Nolin, Godmother: Genevieve Nolin, G. A. Belcourt priest. (page 103)

Gouin, Antoine
    B-669, Antoine Gouin, baptized 29 September 1833, born 27 September 1833, of the

legitimate marriage of Antoine Gouin and Marie Blondeau, Godfather: Louis Blondeau, Godmother: Marie Anne Martin, J. B. Thibault priest. (page 109)

Goulet, Alexis and Josephte Severight
M-110, Alexis Goulet, adult son of Jacques Goulet and Genevieve Begnet, married 1 October 1833, Josephte Severight, minor daughter of John Severight Esq. and Josephte, in the presence of Jacques Goulet & Antoin Gruet, J. N. Ev. de Juliopolis. (page 109)

Goulet, Jacques and Louise Versailles
M-91, Jacques Goulet, adult son of deceased Jacques Goulet and the deceased Genevieve Desmarais, of St-Antoine de la Riviere du Loup, district de Trois-Rivieres, married 3 November 1829, Louise Versailles, adult daughter of Louis Versailles and Madeleine Montagnaise, in the presence of Francois Dubois and Francois Plourde, Jn Harper priest. (page 33-34)

Goulet, Louis
B-675, Louis Goulet, baptized 15 October 1833, born 20 September 1833, of Louis Goulet and Helene Winzel, Godfather: Olivier Charron, Godmother: Angelique Nolin, J. N. Ev de Juliopolis. (page 111)

Goulet, Roger Norbert Alexis
B-833, Roger Norbert Alexis Goulet, baptized 15 August 1834, born this morning of the legitimate marriage of Alexis Goulet and Josephte Severight, Godmother: Marguerite Nolin (signed), J. N. Ev. de Juliopolis. (page 138)

Grant, Anne
B-416, Anne Grant, baptized 11 March 1832, born 8 March 1832, of Cuthbert Grant and Marie McGillia, Godmother: Marguerite Boutineau, F. Boucher priest. (page 59)

Grant, Genevieve
B-777, Genevieve Grant, baptized 5 May 1834, born 2 May 1834, of the legitimate marriage of Jean Baptiste Grant and Julie Ducharme, Godfather: Jean Baptiste Roquebrune, Godmother: Genevieve Lafrance, G. A. Belcourt priest. (page 127)

Grant, Jean Baptiste
B-581, Jean Baptiste Grant, baptized 18 October 1829, born 19 September 1829, of the legitimate marriage of Jean Baptiste Grant, free man, and Julie Ducharme, Godfather: Pierre Parenteau, Godmother: Marguerite De Launais, Fr. Boucher priest. (page 32)

Grant, Marguerite
B-631, Marguerite Grant, baptized 5 August 1833, born yesterday of the legitimate marriage of Cuthbert Grant and Marie McGillis, Godfather: Francois St.Germain, Godmother: Isabelle McGillis, C. E. Poire priest. (page 105)

Grant, Narcisse

B-389, Narcisse, Grant, baptized 15 January 1832, born 4 December 1831, of the mariage of Jean-Baptiste Grant and Julie Ducharme, Godmother: Catherine Nolin, F. Boucher priest. (page 48)

Gregorit, Marguerite

B-147, Marguerite Gregorit, baptized 21 December 1825, born yesterday, of the legitimate marriage of Joseph Gregorit, resident of this mission and Catherine Dubois, Godfather: Christian Warchter, Godmother: Charlotte Marcellet, J. N. Ev. de Juliopolis. (page 21)

Gregovitch, Catherine

B-388, Catherine Gregovitche, baptized 19 January 1832, born of Joseph Gregovitche and Catherine Dubois, Godfather: Jean Yaviche, Godmother: Genevieve Lalonde, G. A. Belcourt priest. (page 48)

Gregovitch, Louis

B-721, Louis Gregovitch, baptized 23 January 1834, born today of the legitimate marriage of Joseph Gregovitch and Catherine Dubois, Godfather: Louis Godon, Godmother: Josephte Dubois, J. B. Thibault priest. (page 126)

Grenon, Gaspard

B-75, Gaspard Grenon, baptized 26 June 1825, age about 7 months, son of Joseph Grenon, free man, and Angelique Folle-Avoine, Godfather: Charles Gaspard Brousse, Godmother: Marguerite Lanoue, Ths. Destroimaisons priest. (page 4)

Grenon, Marguerite

See Alexis Bonami dit Lesperance and Marguerite Grenon

Grouette, Augustin

B-__, Augustin Gruet, baptized 27 November 1833, born this morning, of the legitimate marriage of Antoine Gruet and Magdeleine [Nolin] ... (page 121)

Grouette, Jean Baptiste

B-583, Jean Baptiste Grouette, baptized 18 October 1829, born 8 March, of the legitimate marriage of Antoine Grouette and Magdeleine Nolin, Godfather: Thomas Pivan, Godmother: Marguerite Nolin, Fr. Boucher priest. (page 32)

Grouette, Marguerite

B-392, Marguerite Grouette, baptized 15 January 1832, born 7 January 1832, of the legitimate marriage of Antoine Grouette and Magdeleine Nolin, Godmother: Catherine Nolin, F. Boucher priest. (page 49)

Guiboche, Angelique
> B-537, Angelique Guiboche, baptized 17 February 1833, age 48 years, Godmother: Charlotte Latourelle, C. E. Poire priest. (page 90)

Guiboche, Angelique
> See Joseph Caplet and Angelique Guiboche

Guilbeau, Francoise
> B-561, Francoise Guilbeau, baptized 5 July 1829, age 21 years, daughter of the late Pierre Guilbeau and Angelique, Godmother: Josephte, Widow Harrison, J. N. Ev. de Juliopolis priest. (page 27)

Guilbeau, Francoise
> See George Racette and Francoise Guilbeau

Hallett, Marie
> See Louis Letendre and Marie Hallett

Hamelin, Cecile
> B-695, Cecile Hamelin, baptized 14 November 1833, born yesterday of the legitimate marriage of Louis Hamelin and Cecile Boyer, Godfather: Alexandre Wenzel, Godmother: Marguerite Devis, C. E. Poire priest. (page 116)

Hamelin, Denys
> B-682, Denys Hamelin, baptized 28 October 1833, born yesterday of the legitimate marriage of Jean Baptiste Hamelin and Francoise Ducharme, Godmother: Monique Hamelin, J. B. Thibault priest. (page 112)

Hamelin, Elisabeth
> See Joseph Deganne and Elisabeth Hamelin

Hamelin, Isabelle
> S-51, Isabelle Hamelin, buried 7 December 1833, died yesterday, age 19, wife of Joseph Deganne, in the presence of Louis Gariepy and Jean Baptiste Lepine, J. B. Thibault priest. (page 122)

Hamelin, Marie
> S-47, Marie Hamelin, buried 27 August 1833, died day before yesterday, age 10 years, daughter of Jacques Hamelin and Louise, in the presence of Baptiste Degane and Paul Larente, C. E. Poire priest. (page 106)

Harriett, Robert
B-808, Robert Harriette, baptized 10 July 1834, age 3 months, son of Sieur Harriett and Julie Desjarlais, Godfather: Amable Hogue, Godmother: Angelique Nolin, J. B. Thibault priest. (page 132)

Harrison, Marie
See Jean Baptiste Lagimoniere and Marie Harrison

Heneau, Sophie dit Canada
B-576, Sophie Heneau dit Canada, baptized 6 April 1833, age 15 years, daughter of Charles Heneau dit Canada and Marie Thomas, Godmother: Francoise St.Germain, G. A. Belcourt priest. (page 98)

Heneau, Sophie
See Dominique Charon and Sophie Heneau

Henry, Alexis and Marie Lionnais
M-120, Alexis Henry, adult son of Sieur William Henry and Agathe Letendre, married 26 November 1833, Marie Lionnais, minor daughter of Francois Lionnais and Louise Sauteuse, in the presence of Francois Lionnais and Louis Letendre, G. A. Belcourt priest. (page 121)

Henry, Alexis: B-571, Alexis Henry, baptized 6 April 1833, age 21 years, son of William Henry and Agathe Letendre, Godfather: Louis Letendre, G. A. Belcourt priest. (page 97)

Henry, Louise: B-891, Louise Henry, baptized 16 November 1834, age 33 years, daughter of Sieur Robert Henry and .. (page 154)

Henry, Louise: See Pierre St.Germain and Louise Henry

Herman, Edouard and Marguerite Cris
M-86, Edouard Herman, adult son of Sieur Jacques Herman and Louise Sauteuse, married 8 June 1829, Magdeleine Paquin, minor daughter of Joseph Paquin and Marguerite of the nation of Cris, this marriage was celebrated without the publication of any banns and with a dispensation for disparity of creed in favor of the bride who is infidel and who refused to be baptized, in the presence of Jean Baptiste Pontbrillant and Michel Delaunais, Jn Harper. (page 23)

Herman, Edouard
B-__, Edouard Herman, baptized 8 June 1829, born 25 years the 24 March, son of Jacques Herman, member of the society of the North West, and the deceased Louise Saulteuse, Godfather: Andre Millet, J. N. Ev. de Juliopolis. (page 23)

Hogue, Amable

    B-583, Amable Hogue, baptized 12 May 1833, born 6 May 1833, of the legitimate marriage of Amable Hogue and Marguerite Tailer, Godfather: Louis Galarneau, Godmother: Magdeleine David, C. E. Poire priest. (page 100)

Hogue, Marie

    B-396, Marie Hogue, born 18 January 1832 [sic] X, baptized 12 January 1832 [sic], of the legitmate marriage of Amable Hogue and Marguerite Taylor, Godfather: Andre Gaudry, Godmother: Marguerite Grenon, J. N. Ev. de Juliopolis. (X month before) [born 18 December 1832] (page 51)

Houle, Angelique

    B-137, Angelique Houle, baptized 23 October 1825, born 20 October 1825, of Charles Houle, free man, and Louise Berland, Godfather: Jean Baptiste Latourelle, Godmother: Francoise Beauchamp, Jn Harper priest. (page 17)

Houle, Charles

    B-587, Charles Holl, baptized [between 17 and 22] May 1833, born 13 May 1833, of the legitimate marriage of Antoine Holl and Josephte Lauzon, Godfather: Urbain Delorme, Godmother: Emilie Wels, F. Boucher priest. (page 101)

Houle, Joseph

    B-877, Joseph Houle, baptized 5 October 1834, age 4 months, son of Francois Houle and Magdelaine Lafreniere, Godfather: William Shaw (signed), Godmother: Marie Geo[rge], J. N. Ev de Juliopolis. (page 150)

Houle, Josephte

    B-431, Josephte Hool, baptized 12 May 1832, born 8 May 1832, of the legitimate marriage of William Holl and Josephte Boisvert, Godfather: Pierre Beauchamp, Godmother: Marie Morin, F. Boucher priest. (page 63)

Houle, Josephte

    See Michel Leclerc dit Alard and Josephte Holl

Houle, Marie

    B-846, Marie Houle, baptized 27 August 1834, born 24 August 1834, of the legitimate marriage of William Houle and Josephte Boisvert, Godfather: Pierre Pikle, Godmother: Marie Pikle, J. B. Thibault priest. (page 142)

Houle, Marie

    S-74, Marie Houle, buried 9 September 1834, died this night, age 15 days, daughter of

William Houle and Josephte Boisvert, in the presence of Isidore Bernier and Louis Bousquet, C. E. Poire priest. (page 144)

Hughes, Catherine
	B-875, Catherine Hughes, baptized 30 September 1834, age about 34 years, daughter of Sieur James Hughes and a Corbeau, Godmother: Angelique Dion, J. B. Thibault priest. (page 149)

Hughes, Catherine
	See Louis Berard and Catherine Hughes

Hughes, Charlotte
	B-876, Charlotte Hughes, baptized 30 September 1834, age about 38 years, daughter of Sieur James Hughes and a Corbeau, Godmother: Angelique Nolin, J. B. Thibault priest. (page 149-150)

Huneau, Jean Baptiste
	B-572, Jean Baptiste Huneau, baptized 6 April 1833, age 21 years, son of Michel Huneau and a Sauteuse, Godfather: Antoine Dupuis, G. A. Belcourt priest. (page 97)

Indian, Angelique
	B-836, Angelique, baptized 21 August 1834, age 4 years, daughter of Kekijiwe and Nanjadjin, Godmother: Angelique Nolin, G. A. Belcourt priest. (page 139)

Indian, Angelique
	B-839, Angelique, baptized 21 August 1834, daughter of ..mikak, age 2 years, Godfather: William Shaw (signed), G. A. Belcourt priest. (page 139-140)

Indian, Augustin
	B-841, Augustin, baptized 22 August 1834, age 2 years, son of Jemimeckang-iban and Ojin-kok, Godmother: Angelique Nolin, G. A. Belcourt priest. (page 140)

Indian, Charles
	B-887, Charles, baptized 4 November 1834, born August 1834, son of Tckweyanakwak and ..de-ke-ojock, Godmother: Angelique Nolin, C. E. Poire priest. (page 153)

Indian, Cuthbert
	B-532, Cuthbert, baptized 28 January 1833, age 2 years, born of Indian parents, Godfather: Cuthbert Grant, Godmother: Julie Le Roche Blave, F. Boucher priest. (page 87)

Indian, Francois
	B-620, Francois Indian, baptized 3 March 1830, age about 22 years, Godfather: Augustin Nolin (signed), Fr. Boucher priest. (page 44)

Indian, Genevieve
    B-794, Genevieve, baptized 15 June 1834, age 3 months, daughter of Metwewinin and Nakiik, Godfather: Arsene Morisset, Godmother: Janotte [Genevieve ?] Nolin, J. B. Thibault priest. (page 129)

Indian, Genevieve
    B-577, Genevieve, baptized 7 April 1833, age 5 years, born of Indian parents, Godfather: Francois Desmarais, Godmother: Genevieve Nolin, F. Boucher priest. (page 98)

Indian, infant
    S__, infant Indian, buried 27 December 1831, parents unknown, of the prairie of White Horse Plains, in the presence of Francois Delorme and Pierre Divertissant, F. Boucher priest. (page 47)

Indian, Isabelle
    B-486, Isabelle, baptized 23 August 1832, born today of a female Indian and an unknown father, Godfather: Jean Baptiste Marcelot, Godmother: Marie Desjarlais, F. Boucher priest. (page 73)

Indian, Jean Baptise
    B-840, Jean Baptiste , baptized 22 August 1834, age 7 years, son of Kawice.. and Ojinawabikok, Godmother: Angelique [Nolin ?], G. A. Belcourt priest. (page 140)

Indian, Jean Baptiste
    B-699, Jean Baptiste, baptized 12 November 1833, age about 12 days, son of Mackutebwan and Kijikopinestkkwe, Godfather: Cuthbert Grant Esquire, Godmother: Marguerite Grant, G. A. Belcourt priest. (page 117)

Indian, Joseph
    B__, Joseph Indian, baptized 20 June 1825, age about 8 months, son of Kapinanikapow and Maskopatok, infidels, Godfather: Charles Gaspard Brousse (signed), Godmother: Marguerite Lanoue, Jn Harper priest. (page 3)

Indian, Marie
    B-533, Marie, baptized 28 January 1833, age 4 years, born of Indian parents, Godfather: Drapau [?], Godmother: Isabelle McGillis, F. Boucher priest. (page 87)

Indian, Pierre
    B-894, Pierre, baptized 23 November 1834, age about 6 months, son of .. Otoudakkawekok .. (page 155)

Indian, Pierre

S-55, Pierre Indian, buried 15 February 1830, age 6 years, in the presence of Pierre Diverssant and Ferdinand Sheller,   J. N. Ev. de Juliopolis priest. (page 42)

Isaac, Genevieve

B-477, Genevieve Isaac, baptized 20 September 1832, born this morning, of the legitimate marriage of Michel Isaac and Magdelaine Roy, Godfather: William Shaw (signed), Godmother: Genevieve Savoyard, J. N. Ev de Juliopolis. (page 76)

Isaac, Marie

B-616, Marie Isaac, baptized 22 February 1830, of the legitmate marriage of Michel Isaac and ... [Magdeleine] Roy, Godfather: Joseph Landri, Godmother: Marie .. , Jn Harper priest (page 44)

Janot, Marie Magdelaine

B-553, Marie Magdelaine Janot, baptized 10 March 1833, born today of the legitimate marriage of Jean Baptiste Janot and Louise Roquebrune, Godfather: Jean Baptiste Roquebrune, Godmother: Rosalie Janot, G. A. Belcourt priest. (page 94)

Jerome, Andre

B-595, Andre Jerome, baptized 15 December 1829, born yesterday, of the legitimate marriage of Martin Jerome and Angelique Letendre, Godfather: Andre Carriere, Godmother: Louise Jerome, Jn. Harper priest. (page 36)

Jerome, Joseph

B-481, Joseph Jerome, baptized 19 August 1832, born 1 August 1832, of the legitimate marriage of Martin Jerome, farmer, and Elizabeth Wilkie, Godfather: Joseph Roc, Godmother: Genevieve Lafrance, F. Boucher priest. (page 72)

Jerome, Louis

B-718, Louis Jerome, baptized 20 January 1834, born yesterday of the legitimate marriage of [Martin] Jerome and Bethsy Wilky, Godfather: .. Letendre, Godmother: Julie H... (page 124)

Jerome, Marie-Louise

See Maximilien Genton and Marie-Louise Jerome

Jerome, Martin and Angelique Letendre

M-14, Martin Jerome, adult son of Martin Jerome and an Indian, married 6 June 1825, Angelique Letendre, minor daughter of Jean Baptiste Letendre and Josephte Indian, in the presence of Pierre Versaille and Jean Baptiste Letendre, Ths Destroimaisons priest. (page 2)

Joyal, Toussaint and Marguerite Lapointe

     M-23, Toussaint Joyal, free man, adult son of Toussaint Joyal and Louise Chatel, of Berthier, District of Montreal, married 26 September 1825, Marguerite Lapointe, minor daughter of Antoine Lapointe deceased and Charlotte Lanoue, mother and father of this mission, in the presence of Charles Brousse and Francois Plourde, Ths. Desroismaisons priest. (page 13)

Joyal, Toussaint

     B-670, Toussaint Joyal, baptized 6 October 1833, age one year, son of Toussaint Joyal and Marguerite Lapointe, Godfather: Francois Bruce, Godmother: Emilie Bruce, J. B. Thibault priest. (page 110)

Kekepokkwaneb, Marie

     S-68, Marie Kekepokkwaneb, baptized 22 August 1834, died yesterday, age 3 years, daughter of Kekepokkwaneb and Kepekonibik, in the presence of Charles Montigny and Alexandre Charron dit Ducharme, C. E. Poire priest. (page 140)

Kikepokwaneb, Joseph

     S-60, Joseph Kikepokwaneb, buried 2 July 1834, died day before yesterday, age 30 years, in the presence of Isidore Bernier (signed) and Pierre Carron (signed), G. A. Belcourt priest. (page 130)

Kikikkopinens, Marie

     B-830, Marie Kikikkopinens, baptized 1 July 1834, age 2 months, daughter of Kikikkopinens and Keroyaweskopinens [?], Godfather: Eustache Carron, Godmother: Marguerite, C. E. Poire priest. (page 137)

Kikikkopinens, Marie

     S__, Marie Kekekkopinens, buried 5 July 1834 on the prairie, age 2 months and 5 days, daughter of Kekekkopinens and de wijaweekopinens. in the presence of Jean Baptiste Wilky and Joseph Vallee, C. E. Poire priest. (page 137)

Kilcool, Marie

     B-564, Marie Kilcool, baptized 20 July 1829, born yesterday, of the legitimate marriage of Denis Kilcoot and Cecile Turpin, Godfather: Andre Gaudry, Godmother: Isabelle Normand, Jn Harper priest. (page 28)

Kilcool, Marie

     S-48, Marie Kilcool, buried 22 July 1829, died yesterday age - days, daughter of Denis Kilcool and Cecile Turpin, Godfather: Antoine Caron and Alexandre Macdonell, Jn. Harper priest. (page 28)

St.Boniface Register 1825-1834 (Saved From The Fire)

Kilkook, Marguerite
> B-884, Marguerite Kilkool, baptized 22 October 1834, born 16 October 1834, of the legitimate marriage of Michel Kilkool and Cecile Turpen, Godfather: Pierre Goulet, Godmother: Marguerite Dease, J. B. Thibault priest. (page 152)

L'Heureaux, Francois
> B-151, Francois L'Heureux, baptized 18 December 1825, Winnipeg River, age 3 years, son of Francois L'Heureux and a Mandan, Godfather: Joseph Dagneau, Godmother: Genevieve Cameron, Ths. Destroismaisons priest. (page 22)

La Serpante, Louis
> B-631, Louis La Serpante, baptized 21 March 1830, the father and mother unknown, Godfather: Jean Baptiste Fagnan, Godmother: Magdeleine wife of Ferdinand Scheller, Jn Harper priest. (page 46)

Labissoniere, Elmire
> B-592, Elmire Labissoniere, baptized 29 November 1829, born day before yesterday, of the legitimate marriage of Joseph Labissoniere and Francoise Desjarlais, Godfather: Mr. John Bourke (signed John P. Bourke), Godmother: Marie-Anne Gaboury, Fr. Boucher priest. (page 35)

Labissonniere, Felicite
> B-714, Felicite Labissonniere, baptized 7 January 1834, born this morning of the legitimate of Joseph Labissonniere and Francoise Desjarlais, Godfather: Jean Baptiste Boisvert.... (page 123)

Lacerte, Marguerite
> B-667, Marguerite Lacerte, baptized 23 September 1833, born today of the legitimate marriage of Louis Lacerte and Josephte Martin, Godfather: Antoine Dupuis, Godmother: Susanne Laurin, J. B. Thibault priest. (page 109)

Lacourse, Genevieve
> See Antoine Legault dit Deslauriers and Genevieve Lacourse

Lacouture, Josephte
> B-600, Josephte Lacouture, baptized 26 May 1833, age 7 months, daughter of Jean Baptiste [Ledoux] and Francoise Lacouture, Godfather Ant.... (page 103)

Ladouceur, Bazile
> B-816, Bazile Ladouceur, baptized 13 July 1834, age 7 years, son of Joseph Ladouceur and [Josephte] Lapierre, Godfather: Louis Larrive, Godmother: Angelique Laliberte, J. B. Thibault priest. (page 134)

Ladouceur, Julie
    B-817, Julie Ladouceur, baptized 13 July 1834, age 5 years, daughter of Joseph Ladouceur and Josephte Lapierre, Godfather: Thomas Pevin, Godmother: Tharese Belanger, J. B. Thibault priest. (page 134)

Ladoucur, Olivier
    B-815, Olivier Ladouceur, baptized 13 July 1834, age 2 years, daughter of Joseph Ladouceur and Josephte Lapierre, Godfather: Jean Baptiste Moreau, Godmother: Charlotte Lafeuille, J. B. Thibault priest. (page 134)

Laferte, Louis and Angelique Caron
    M-114, Louis Laferte, adult son of the late Joseph Laferte and Marie Goyette of Yamaska, married 12 November 1833, Angelique Caron, minor daughter of Antoine Caron and Angelique St.Germain, in the presence of Guillaume Rocheleau, Amable Branconnier, and Alexandre Wenzel, C. E. Poire priest. (page 115-116)

Laferte, Louis
    B-819, Louis Laferte, baptized 23 July 1834, born this night of the legitimate marriage of Louis Laferte and Angelique Carron, Godfather: Antoine Carron, Godmother: Catherine Morin, J. B. Thibault priest. (page 135)

Laferte, Louis
    S-70, Louis Laferte, buried 26 August 1834, died yesterday, age one month, son of Louis Laferte and Angelique Carron, in the presence of Antoine Carron and .. Carron, C. E. Poire priest. (page 141)

Lafleur, Joseph Pelle dit and Louise Belanger
    M-119, [Joseph Pelle dit Lafleur ?], son of the late Louis Pelle dit [LaFleur Cris ?] and the deceased Marianne ..., married 26 November 1833, Louise Belanger, minor daughter of Louis Belanger and Josephte Daze, in the presence of Ignace Mac Donell and Louis Belanger, G. A. Belcourt priest. (page 120-121)

Lafond, Jean Baptiste
    B-400, Jean Baptiste Lafond, baptized 19 February 1832, age 25 days, legitimate son of Amable Lafond and Marie Racette, Godfather: Joseph Amelin, Godmother: Elizabeth Henry, J. V. Ev. de Juliopolis priest. (page 52)

Lafont, Joseph
    B-885, Joseph Lafont, baptized 27 October 1834, born this night of the legitimate marriage of Amable Lafont and Marie Racette, Godfather: Pierre Carron, Godmother: Francoise Sauteuse, J. B. Thibault priest. (page 152)

St.Boniface Register 1825-1834 (Saved From The Fire)

Lafont, Magdeleine
     B-584, Magdeleine Lafont, baptized 25 October 1829, age about 2 [?], legitimate daughter of Amable Lafont and Marie Racette, Godfather: __ Goulet, Godmother: Euphrosine Garriepy, Jn Harper priest. (page 32)

Lafontaine, Jean Baptiste and Marie de Rocheblave
     M-15, Jean Baptiste Lafontaine, free man, adult son of Jean Baptiste Lafontaine and a Sioux, married 6 June 1825, Marie de Rocheblave, adult daughter of of Pie... [Pierre] Rocheblave esquire and a Sauteuse, in the presence of Alexis Bonami and Benjamin Marchand, Ths Destroismaisons priest (page 2)

Lafournaise, Jean Baptiste
     B-480, Jean Baptiste Lafournaise, baptized 19 August 1832, born 13 July last, of the legitimate marriage of Jean Baptiste Lafournaise and Marguerite Gosselin, Godfather: Joseph Lafournaise, Godmother: Marguerite Lafournaise, F. Boucher priest. (page 72)

Lafournaise, Joseph and Susanne Leclerc
     M-98, Joseph Lafournaise, adult son of the deceased Mathurin Lafournaise and the deceased Archange Lalonde, the mother and father lived at Montreal, married 8 February 1830, Susanne Leclerc, adult daughter of the deceased Leclerc and a Carcie, in the presence of Joseph Parenteau and Joseph Decoteau, Fr. Boucher priest. (page 39)

Lafournaise, Marguerite
     B-604, Marguerite Lafournaise, baptized [7] February 1830, age about 15 years, daughter of Joseph Lafournaise and Susanne Leclair, Godmother: Emilie Parenteau, Fr. Boucher priest. (page 39)

Lafournaise, Marie-Anne
     See Joseph Decoteau and Marie-Anne Lafournaise

Lafreniere, Joseph
     B-601, Joseph Lafreniere, baptized 26 May 1833, 3 weeks, legitimate daughter of Antoine Lafreniere and Marguerite Houle, Godfather: Etienne McGillis, Godmother: Josephte Latour, C. E. Poire priest. (page 104)

Lagimoniere, Benjamin and Angelique Carrier
     M-123, Benjamin Lagimoniere, adult son of Jean Baptiste Lagimoniere and Marie Anne Gabouri, married 21 January 1834, Angelique Carrier, minor daughter of Andre Carrier and Angelique Dion, in the presence of Jean Baptiste Lagimoniere and Andre Carrier, J. N. Ev. de Juliopolis. (page 125)

St.Boniface Register 1825-1834 (Saved From The Fire)

Lagimoniere, Jean Baptiste and Marie Harrison

M-87, Jean Baptiste Lagimoniere, adult son of Jean Baptiste Lagimoniere and Marie-Anne Gabouri of this mission, married 8 June 1829, Marie Harrison, adult daughter of the late Sieur Thomas Harrison and Josephte Crie, in the presence of Jean Baptiste Lagimoniere, father of the groom, and Francois Charon, Jn. Harper priest. (page 23)

Lagimoniere, Joseph

B-146, Joseph Lagimoniere, baptized 20 December 1825, born today, of the legitmate marriage of Jean Baptiste Lagimoniere, resident of this mission, and Marie Anne Gabouri, Godfather: Jean Baptiste Lagimoniere, brother of the infant, Godmother: Josephte Lagimoniere, Jn Haprper priest. (page 21)

Lagimoniere, Marguerite

B-536, Marguerite Lagimoniere, baptized 11 February 1833, born yesterday of the legitimate marriage of Jean Baptiste Lagimoniere and Marie Harrison, Godfather: Thomas Harrison, Godmother: Apolline Lagimoniere, F. Boucher priest. (page 88)

Lagimoniere, Moyse

B-627, Moyse Lagimoniere, baptized 5 April 1830, born this morning of the legitimate marriage of Jean Baptiste Lagimoniere and Marie Harrisson, Godfather: Jean Baptiste Lagimoniere, Godmother: Josephte ... Grandfather and grandmother of the infant, J. N. Ev. de Juliopolis priest (page 45)

Laliberte, Angelique

B-118, Angelique Laliberte, baptized 25 September 1825, age 15 years, daughter of Pierre Laliberte, resident of this mission, and Joseph Baudry, Godmother: Marguerite Grenon, Ths. Destroismaisons priest. (page 12)

Laliberte, Angelique

See Joseph Vermet and Angelique Laliberte

Lalonde, Jean Baptiste

B-148, Jean Baptiste Lalonde, baptized 28 December 1825, born yesterday, of the legitimate marriage of Jean Baptiste Lalonde and Catherine Nadeau, Godfather: Louis Mersant, Godmother: Josephte Marleau, J. N. Ev de Juliopolis priest. (page 22)

Lambert, Antoine and Marie Sauteuse

M-69, Antoine Lambert, adult son of Jacques Lambert and the late ... Danis, of St.Michel, Yamaska, married 9 May 1832 Marie Sauteuse, in the presence of Francois Bruneau (signed) and Jean Yanche, G. A. Belcourt priest. (page 62)

St.Boniface Register 1825-1834 (Saved From The Fire)

Lambert, Etienne and Catherine Gaudy
    M-70, Etienne Lambert, adult son of Jaques Lambert and the deceased Louise Danis of Yamaska in Canada, and Catherine Gaudy, a Protestant becoming a Catholic, in the presence of Joseph Pilon and Francois Bruneau, G. A. Belcourt priest. (page 62-63)

Lambert, Etienne
    B-549, Etienne Lambert, baptized 5 March 1833, born 26 February 1833, of the legitimate marriage of Etienne Lambert and Catherine Gawdy, Godfather: Jean Baptiste Larance, Godmother: Louise Montagnaise, G. A. Belcourt priest. (page 94)

Lamirande, Louis and Marguerite Danis
    M-102, Louis Lamirande, adult son of Jacques Lamirande and Marie Anne Hebert of the parish of Saint Francois, Three Rivers District, married 19 February 1833, Marguerite Danis, adult daughter of the late Jean Baptiste Danis and Marguerite Lambert, in the presence of Jean Baptiste Versail and Joseph Caplet, F. Boucher priest. (page 92)

Landry, Anastasie
    B-453, Anastasie Landry, baptized 28 June 1832, born yesterday of the legitimate marriage of Joseph Landry and Genevieve Lalonde, Godfather: Michel Monet dit Belhumeur, Godmother: Josephte Dubois, G. A. Belcourt priest. (page 69)

Landry, Jean Baptiste
    B-553, Jean Baptiste Landry, baptized 21 June 1829, born yesterday, of the legitimate marriage of Joseph Landry and Genevieve Lalonde, Godfather: Charles Larence, Godmother: Genevieve Lacourse, J. N. Ev. de Juliopolis priest. (page 25)

Landry, Louis and Anne Martin
    M-100, Louis Landry, adult son of Julien Landry and the deceased Josephte Montagnaise, married 18 February 1833, Anne Martin, adult daughter of Joseph Martin and a Sauteuse, in the presence of Andre Carriere and Antoine Dupuis, witnesses, F. Boucher priest. (page 91)

Landry, Louis and Isabelle Chalifoux
    M-96, Louis Landry, adult son of Louis Landry and Louise Decotes, publication at St.Francois Xavier, White Horse Plains, married 11 February 1833, Isabelle Chalifoux, widow of Antoine Pegman, in the presence of Ambroise Alard and Francois Cyr, G. A. Belcourt priest. (page 88-89)

Landry, Louis
    B-427, Louis Landry, baptized 22 April 1832, age 25 years, son of Louis Landry and Louise Descote, Godfather: Angus McGillis, G. A. Belcourt priest. F. Boucher priest. (page 61)

Landry, Louis

     B-478, Louis Landry, baptized 19 August 1832, age three years last 29 June, son of Louis Landry and Anne Martin, Godfather: Jean Baptiste Frederic, Godmother: Josephte Bourret, J. N. Ev. de Juliopolis priest. (page 72)

Landry, Marie

     B-479, Marie Landry, baptized 19 August 1832, Marie Landry, born 2 February last, daughter of Louis Landry and Annie Martin, Godfather: Andre Millet, Godmother: Francoise Saint Germain, F. Boucher priest. (page 72)

Landry, Marie Madelaine

     B-546, Marie Magdelaine Landry, baptized 24 February 1833, age 9 years, daughter of Louis Landry and Marie Anne Martin, Godmother: Angelique Carron, G. A. Belcourt priest. (page 93)

Landry, Theophile

     B-694, Theophile Landry, baptized 12 November 1833, born 9 November 1833, of the legitimate marriage of Joseph Landry and Genevieve, Godfather: Antoine Vandal, Godmother: Isabelle Lambert, J. B. Thibault priest. (page 116)

Langis, Antoine

     B-446, Antoine Langis, baptized 14 June 1832, born 20 May 1832, Francois Langis and Marguerite George, Godfather: Francois Bruneau (signed), Godmother: Amable Azure, G. A. Belcourt priest. (page 67)

Lanoue, Charlotte

     See Joseph Descoteaux and Charlotte Lanoue

Lapointe, Marguerite

     B-119, Marguerite Lapointe, baptized 25 September 1825, age 15 years on 26 February, of Antoine Lapointe and Charlotte Lanoue, Godmother: Josephte Sauteuse, Ths. Destroismaisons priest. (page 12)

Lapointe, Marguerite

     See Toussaint Joyal and Marguerite Lapointe

Larence, Josephte

     S-75, Josephte Larence, buried 14 September 1834, daughter of [Charles] Larence and Josephte Desjardins, in the presence of Amable Nault and Pierre Carron, J. B. Thibault priest. (page 144-145)

Larence, Julie
      S-78, Julie Larence, buried 10 November 1834, died yesterday, age 3 years and 2 months, daughter of Charles Larence and Josephte Desjardins, in the presence of Amable N[ault] and Benjamin Gervais, J. B. Thibault priest. (page 154)

Larence, Moyse
      B-710, Moyse Larence, baptized 19 December 1833, born this morning of the legitimate marriage of Charles Larence and Josephte Desjardins, Godfather: Amable .., Godmother: Marie Anne Gabouri, J. N. Ev de Juliopolis. (page 122)

Lariviere, Angelique
      See Francois Dubois and Angelique Lariviere

Lariviere, Cecile
      B-674, Cecile Lariviere, baptized 15 October 1833, age about two years, daughter of Pierre Lariviere and Helene Winzel, Godfather: Oliver Charron, Godmother: Angelique Nolin, J. N. ev. de Juliopolis. (page 111)

Larock, Marguerite
      B-420, Marguerite Larock, baptized 14 April 1832, born 9 April 1832, of the legitimate marriage of Charles Larock and Catherine Macon, Godfather: Andre Millet, Godmother: Genevieve Lafra..., J. N. Ev. de Julipolis priest. (page 60)

Larocque, Marguerite
      B-76, Marguerite Larocque, baptized 3 July 1825, age about one month, daughter of Olivier Larocque, free man, and Magdelaine Picher, Godfather: Jeremie Ledeux, Godmother: Marguerite .., Jn Harper priest. (page 4)

Laronde, Louis
      B-95, Louis Laronde, baptized 7 August 1825, born - July last, of the legitimate marriage of __ Laronde and Magdelaine Boucher, Godfather: Jean Baptiste Peleau, Godmother: __ Rocheblave, J. N. Harper priest. (page 8)

Laroque, Josephte
      B-591, Josephte Laroque, baptized 25 November 1829, born today, of the legitimate marriage of Charles Laroque and Catherine Macon, Godfather: Jean-Baptiste Laderoute, Godmother: Josephte Rocbrune, Frs. Boucher priest. (page 35)

Laroque, Magdeleine
      B-834, Magdeleine Laroque, baptized 18 August 1834, born today of the legitimate marriage of Charles Laroque and (Catherine) Macon, Godfather: William Shaw (signed), Godmother: Marguerite Laframboise, J... (page 138)

Laroque, Pierre
    B-889, Pierre Laroque, baptized 12 November 1834, born yesterday of the legitimate marriage of [Pierre] Laroque and Genevieve Savoyard, Godfather: Joseph Savoyard, Godmother: Marie, J. B. Thibault priest. (page 154)

Latour, Jean Baptiste
    S-8, Jean Baptiste Latour, buried 4 November 1825, died day before yesterday, age about 36 years, in the presence of Pierre Divertissant and Jeremie Leduc, Ths. Destroismaisons priest. (page 18)

Lavallee, Joseph
    B-621, Joseph Lavallee, baptized 14 March 1830, age about 19 years, daughter of Louis Lavallee and an Assiniboine, Godfather: Pierre Parenteau, Frs. Boucher. priest (page 44)

Lavallee, Louise
    B-565, Louise Lavallee, baptized 22 July 1829, born yesterday, of Louis Lavallee, free man of this mission, and Louise Martel, Godfather: Andre Carriere, Godmother: Angelique Dion, Jn. Harper priest. (page 28)

Lavallee, Marguerite
    B-436, Marguerite Lavalle, baptized 21 May 1832, age 32 years, daughter of Ignace Lavalle and Josephte, Godmother: Marie Fortin, F. Boucher priest. (page 65)

Lavallee, Marguerite
    See Paul Paul and Marguerite Lavallee

Leberge, Marie Anne
    B-719, Marie Anne Leberge, baptized 22 January 1834, born today of the legitimate marriage of Michel Leberge and Madeleine Vivier, Godfather: Pierre Parenteau, Godmother: Marie Anne Martin, J. B. Thibault priest. (page 126)

Leblanc, Henriette
    B-512, Henriette Le Blanc, baptized 27 December 1832, born 7 November 1832, of the legitimate marriage of Pierre Le Blanc (signed) and [Nancy] McKenzie, Godfather: Guillaume Fournier, Godmother: Marguerite Nolin. (page 86)

LeClair, Ambroise dit Alard and Louise Decoste
    M-60, Ambroise Le Clair dit Alard, (publication at St.Francois Xavier of White Horse Plains) adult son of Ambroise Le Clair dit Alard and Charlotte of the Cris, married 29 February 1832 Louise Decoste, adult daughter of Francois Decoste and a Masquegone, in the presence of Joseph Arcand and Jean Baptiste Paul, G. A. Belcourt priest. (page 54-55)

Leclerc, Ambroise dit Alard
      B-697, Ambroise Leclerc dit Alard, baptized 20 September 1833, born 17 September 1833, of the legitimate marriage of Ambroise Leclerc dit Alard Jr., and Marguerite Chalifoux, Godfather: Ambroise Leclerc Sr., Godmother: Isabelle Collin, G. A. Belcourt priest. (page 117)

Leclerc, Michel
      B-439, Michel Leclerc, baptized 2 June 1832, age about 20 years, child of Ambroise Leclerc and a Sauteuse, Godfather: Angus McGillis, F. Boucher priest. (page 66)

Leclerc, Michel dit Alard and Josephte Houle
      M-105, Michel Leclerc dit Alard, adult son of Ambroise Leclerc dit Alard, married 29 April 1833, Josephte Holl, minor daughter of Antoine Holl and Josephte Lauson, in the presence of Ambroise Leclerc and Antoine Houlle, Boucher priest. (page 100)

Leclerc, Susanne
      See Joseph Lafournaise and Susanne Leclerc

Ledoux, Eusebe and Susanne Bonneau
      M-79, Eusebe Le Doux adult son of Jean Baptiste Le Doux and Magdelaine Sauteuse, married at St.Francois Xavier of White Horse Plains on 8 October 1832, Susanne Bonneau, minor daughter of Jean Baptiste Bonneau and Marie, in the presence of Joseph Guilbeau and Louis Gariepi, G. A. Belcourt priest. (page 79)

Ledoux, Magdelaine
      B-496, Magdelaine Ledoux, baptized 11 November 1832, born 5 November 1832, daughter of Pierre Ledoux and Susan Short, Godfather: Pierre Divertissant dit Falcond, Godmother: Marguerite Ross, G. A. Belcourt priest. (page 81)

Ledoux, [possibly Elmire]
      B__, __ daughter of Jean Baptiste Le Doux and Magdelaine Sauteuse, baptized [between 1 October 1832 and 8 October 1832], Godfather: Antoine Faignant, Godmother: Josephte Grant, G. A. Belcourt priest. (page 79)

Legros, Josephte
      B-594, Josephte Legros, baptized 8 December 1829, born yesterday, of the legitimate marriage of Antoine Legros and Louise Huneau, Godfather: Joseph Parenteau, Godmother: Marguerite, wife of Joseph Parenteau, Jn. Harper priest. (page 36)

Lemagre, Jean Baptiste Kabakated
      B-485, Jean Baptiste Lemagre Kabakated, baptized 16 October 1832, born last month, of Kabakated (Lemagre) and Kenensikwe Saulteux, Godfather: Jean Yanche, Godmother: Angelique

Nolin, J. N. Ev de Juliopolis. (page 78)

Lemai, Angelique
    B-413, Angelique Lemai, baptized 5 March 1832, daughter of Joseph Lemai and Louise Montagnaise, age about 34 years, Godmother: Josephte, G. A. Belcourt priest. (page 58)

Lemai, Angelique
    See Antoine Pilon and Angelique Lemai

Lemaigne, Angelique
    B-613, Angelique Lemaigne, baptized 18 February 1830, age about 2 months, daughter of of a sauvage named Dumaigne, Godmother: Janotte Nolin, F. Boucher priest. (page 42)

Lemaigne, Genevieve
    B-625, Genevieve Lemaigne, baptized 30 March 1830, age about 3 years, Godfather: Pierre Laroque, Godmother: Angelique Nolin, F. Boucher priest. (page 45)

Lemire, Magdeleine
    See Francois Fagnand and Magdeleine Lemire

Lepine, Adelaide [probably]
    B-494, Adelaide __ [Adelaide Lepine daughter of Jean Baptiste Lepine and Julie Henry ?], baptized 5 November 1832, born yesterday, of __, Godfather: Martin Jerome, Godmother: Elisabeth Henney, F. Boucher priest. (page 80-81)

Lesperance, Alexis Bonami dit and Marguerite Grenon
    M-16, Alexis Bonami dit Lesperance, engage of the Hudson Bay Company, adult son of the late Pierre Bonami and the deceased Marguerite Aucoin of Sorel, married 6 June 1825, Mar... Grenon, adult daughter of the late Joseph Grenon and a Sauteuse, in the presence of Joseph Delaunay and Benjamin Marchand, Ths. Destrroismaisons priest (page 2)

Lesperance: See Bonami

Letendre, Angelique
    See Martin Jerome and Angelique Letendre

Letendre, Jean Baptiste and Marguerite Delaunay
    M-11, Jean Baptiste Letendre adult son of Jean Baptiste Letendre, farmer, and Josephte Indienne, married 6 June 1825, Marguerite Delaunay minor daughter of Francois Delaunay, farmer, and Louise Indienne, of St.Boniface, in the presence of Jean Baptiste Letendre and Francois Delaunay father of the bride. Ths Destroismaisons priest. (page 1)

Letendre, Josephte
    B-593, Josephte Letendre, baptized 6 December 1829, born the same day, of the legitimate marriage of Louis Letendre, resident of this mission, and Marie Hallett, Godfather: Jacques Cardinal, Godmother: Marie Letendre, Jn. Harper priest. (page 35)

Letendre, Josephte
    See Pierre Versailles and Josephte Letendre

Letendre, Louis and Marie Hallett
    M-12, Louis Letendre, adult son of J. Baptiste Letendre and Josephte Indian of St.Boniface, married 6 June 1825, Marie Hallett, minor daughter of of Sieur Henry Hallett and Catherine, in the presence of Jean Baptiste Letendre, father, and Martin Jerome, Ths. Destroismaisons priest. (page 1)

Letendre, Louis
    B-487, Louis Letendre, baptized 2 September 1832, born yesterday, of the legitimate marriage of Louis Letendre and Marie Aleck, Godfather: Martin Jerome, Godmother: Helen McMallen, G. A. Belcourt priest. (page 74)

Letendre, Marie
    B-499, Marie Letendre, baptized 23 November 1832, born this morning of the legitimate marriage of Jean Baptiste Letendre and Marguerite Lionnais, Godfather: Francois Lionnais, Godmother: Louise, his wife, J. N. Ev de Juliopolis. (page 82)

Letendre, Stanislas
    B-837, Stanislas Letendre, baptized 21 August 1834, born this morning of the legitimate marriage of Jean Baptiste Letendre and Marguerite Lyonnais, Godfather: William Shaw (signed), Godmother: Susanne Leclerc, J. B. Thibault priest. (page 139)

Lionay, Isabelle
    See Louis Tifau and Isabelle Lionay

Lionnais, Marie
    See Alexis Henry and Marie Lionnais

Lisée, Josephte
    B-117, Josephte Lisée, baptized 25 September 1825, age 14 years the 4th October last, daughter of Antoine Lisée, free man of St.Boniface, and Madelaine Sauteuse, Godmother: Anne Henri.... [Anne Henriette Tait], Ths Destroismaisons priest. (page 12)

Lucier, Toussaint
    B-447, Toussaint Lucier, baptized 17 June 1832, born 8 June 1832, of Toussaint Lucier

and Josephte Lachevretiere, Godfather: Francois Brousse, Godmother: Suzanne Bourre, G. A. Belcourt priest. (page 67)

Macdonald, John
S-29, John Macdonald, buried 25 April 1832, died in the night, age 60. (page 60)

MacDonell, Jean
B-148, Jean MacDonell, baptized 27 December 1825, born 22 December 1825, of the legitimate marriage of Alexandre MacDonnel, Esquire, and Marie MacDonell, Godmother: Miss Isabelle MacDonell, we undersigned priest are the Godfather, Jn. Harper. (page 21)

Machekgone, Louise
B-581, Louise Machekgone, baptized 17 April 1833, age 50 years, daughter of Misassis Machekegone and Mayakamiyom Machekgone, Godmother: Marie, wife of Francois Lambert, C. E. Poire priest. (page 99)

Machkegone, Louise
See Antoine Marsan dit Lapierre and Louise Machkegone

Maillou, Josephte
B-130, Josephte Maillou, baptized 16 October 1825, age 30 years, daughter of Antoine Maillou and a Sarcie, Godmother: Angelique Nolin, J. N. Ev de Juliopolis. (page 16)

Maillou, Josephte
See Joseph Ritchot and Josephte Maillou

Mainville, Augustin, Louise Rivets, Marie Sinclair and Angele Roussile
B__, baptized 21 August 1833 at Rainy Lake, Augustin Mainville, age 2 years, son of Francois Mainville and a Sauteuse, Louise Rivets, age one year and 5 months, daughter of Louis Rivets and Josephte Jourdain, Marie, age one year and 6 months, daughter of William Sinkler and Marie McKay, Angele, age 6 years, daughter of Augustin Roussile and __, Godfather of the four children: William Bouk (signed), Frs. Boucher priest. (page 107)

Malaterre, Angelique
See Francois Delorme and Angelique Malaterre

Malaterre, Charlotte
B-486, Charlotte Malaterre, baptized 1 October 1832, born 30 September 1832, of the legitimate marriage of Jean Baptiste Malaterre and Ange.. Adam, of White Horse Prairie, Godfather: Francois Bruneau, Godmother: Marguerite, G. A. Belcourt priest. (page 78)

St.Boniface Register 1825-1834 (Saved From The Fire)

Marchand, Guillaume
    B-536, Guillaume Marchand, baptized 13 February 1833, born in the night of the legitimate marriage of Benjamin Marchand and Marguerite Nadeau, Godfather: Guillaume Fournier, Godmother: Genevieve Benoit, J. N. Ev. de Juliopolis. (page 89)

Marchand, Julie
    See Louis Carriere and Julie Marchand

Marchand, Marguerite
    See Francois Bouvet and Marguerite Marchand

Marion, Edouard and Elise
    B-878, 879, baptized 13 October 1834, Edouard Marion, born 25 January 1834, Elise Marion, born 8 December 1831, of Narcisse Marion and Marie Boucher, Edouard's Godfather: Pierre St.Germain, Godmother: Angelique Carron, Elise's Godfather: Francois Marion, Godmother: Genevieve Lacourse, J. N. Ev de Juliopolis. (page 151)

Marsan, Antoine dit Lapierre
    M-104, Antoine Marsan dit La Pierre, adult son of Pierre Marsan dit Lapierre and the late Louise Charon of St.Cuthbert, married 17 April 1833, Louise Machkegone, in the presence of Antoine Gouin and Louis Galarneau, F. Boucher priest. (page 99)

Marsant, Euphrosine dit Lapierre
    B-399, Euphrosine Marsant dit Lapierre, baptized 17 February 1832, born yesterday of Antoine Marsant dit Lapierre and Louisa .., Godfather: Abraham Martin, Godmother: Euphrosine Gariepy, J. N. Ev. de Juliopolis priest. (page 52)

Marsolet, Archange
    See Antoine Villebrun and Archange Marsolet

Marsolet, Marie
    B-672, Marie Marsolet, baptized 14 October 1833, born this night of the legitimate marriage of Jean Baptiste Marsolet and M. Wilky, Godfather: Jean Baptiste Wilky, Godmother: Marie Marsolet, J. N. Ev de Juliopolis. (page 110)

Martel, Jean Baptiste and Marguerite Dion
    M-70, Jean Baptiste Martel, adult son of the deceased Joseph Martel and the deceased Josephte Laneville of the parish of Becancour, married 8 May 1832, Marguerite Dion adult daughter of the deceased Joseph Dion and a Crise, in the presence of Jean Morin and Andre Carriere who could not sign.   F. Boucher priest. (page 62)

Martel, Jean Baptiste

     B-563, Jean Baptiste Martel, baptized 6 April 1833, age about twenty-three years, son of Jean Baptiste Martel and Marguerite Dion, Godfather: Louis Carriere, G. A. Belcourt priest. (page 96)

Martin, Angelique

     B-805, Angelique Martin, baptized 10 July 1834, born yesterday of the legitimate marriage of Joseph Martin and Angelique Lapointe, Godfather: Vital Turcotte, Godmother: Magdeleine Ca[plette ?].   J. B. Thibault priest. (page 132)

Martin, Angelique

     S-65, Angelique Martin, buried 15 August 1834, age one month, died yesterday, daughter of Joseph Martin and Angelique Lapointe, in the presence of Charles Montigny and Andre Millet, C. E. Poire priest. (page 138)

Martin, Anne

     B-540, Anne Martin, baptized 17 February 1833, age 31 years, Godmother: Genevieve Benoit, C. E. Poire priest. (page 90)

Martin, Anne

     See Louis Landry and Anne Martin

Martin, Joseph

     B-572, 26 August 1829, baptized Joseph Martin, born during the night of the legitimate marriage of Joseph Martin, resident, and Angelique Pl[ante], Godfather: Louis Marcant, Godmother: Angelique Godon who could not sign.   The father was absent.   + J. N. Ev. de Juliopolis (page 30)

Martin, Paul

     B-508, Paul Martin, baptized 16 December 1832, born day before yesterday of the legitimate marriage of Joseph Martin and Angelique Plante, Godfather: Prospere Chorette, Godmother: Genevieve Cardinal, J. N. Ev de Juliopolis. (page 85)

Martin, Simon, Laurent-Etienne, Marie and Francoise

     B-96 thru 99: Simon, Laurent-Etienne, Marie, and Francoise, baptized 7 August 1825, Simon, age 4 years, Laurent-Etienne, age one on the 22nd of __ - last, Marie, age 6, Francoise, age 3 on the 20th April last, children of Jean Francois Regis Martin, resident of this mission, and Marguerite Racette, Godfather: Francois D__me (Delorme?) And Godmother: Lucile Ducharme, Ths Destroismaisons priest. (page 8)

Matthieu, Aimmee

     B-107, Aimmee Matthieu, baptized 10 September 1825, born yesterday of the legitimate marriage of Alexandre Matthieu and Euphrosine Lecuyer, Godfather: .. Graton, Godmother: Magdelaine David, Ths Destroismaisons priest. (page 10)

McDermot, Henry

B-435, Henry McDermot, baptized 19 May 1832, born day before yesterday, of the legitimate marriage of Henry McDermot and Saly McNaham, Godmother: Helene Cameron, G. A. Belcourt priest. (page 64)

McDonald, Catherine

B-149, Catherine McDonald, baptized 18 December 1825, at Bas of the Winnipeg River, born 9 October 1825, of the legitimate marriage of John McDonald, Esquire, and Marie Potras, Godfather: Joseph Dagneau, Godmother: Genevieve Cam.., Ths. Destroismaisons priest. (page 22)

McDonald, Jean and Marie Cris

M-25, Jean McDonald, free man of this mission, adult son of the late Jean McDonald and Amable Baudoin, of Terrebonne, District of Montreal, married 11 October 1825, Marie of the nation of Cris, in the presence of Angus McDonald and Joseph Allie, Ths. Destroismaisons priest. (page 15)

McDugal, Jean

B-673, Jean McDugal, baptized 15 October 1833, age about 5 years, son of Duncan McDugal and Helene Einzel, Godfather: Oliver Charon, Godmother: Angelique Nolin, J. N. Ev de Juliopolis. (page 111)

McGillis, Angus and Marguerite Sauteux

M-94, Angus McGillis, farmer of this mission, adult son of [Donald] McGillis and the deceased Marie McDonell of Glengarry, married 11 January 1830, Marguerite Sauteux, Present Joseph Guilbeault and Francois Fagnan friends of the groom, Jn. Harper priest. (page 36-37)

McGillis, Donald and Julie Rocheblave

M-95, Donald McGillis adult son of Angus McGillis and Marguerite Sauteuse, the father and mother of this mission, married 11 January 1830, Julie Rocheblave, widow of Jean Bte. Boucher, in the presence of Joseph Page and Louis Guarriepy who could not sign. Jn Harper priest. (page 37)

McGillis, Marguerite

B-507, Marguerite McGillis, baptized 5 December 1832, born yesterday of Alexandre McGillis and Marguerite Boutinau, Godfather: Cuthbert Grant, Godmother: Marguerite Grant, F. Boucher priest. (page 85)

McGillivray, Fredric and __

B-452, Frederic and ... McGillov...baptized 21 June 1832, Frederic age 4 years and ... age

2 years (July), infants of Simon McGillov..., Godfather: Louis Carriere. (page 68)

McIntosh, Archibald, Isabelle Faris, and Nancy Fontaine
        B-688, 689, 690, baptized 1 September 1833, Archi McIntoch, born 22 June 1833, son of Jean McIntoch and Charlotte Robinson, Isabelle Faris, born 9 January 1833, daughter of Marie Faris, Nancy Fontaine, born 27 October 1832, daughter of Joseph Fontaine and Angelique Fagnant, Godfather of the three children: Donald Mcintoch, Godmother: Charlotte Read, Frs. Boucher priest. (page 115)

McIntosh, John and Charlotte Robertson
        M__, John McIntosh (signed), of the Hudson Bay Company, adult son of Donald McIntosh Esquire and Josephte Sauteuse, married 11 July 1834, Charlotte Robertson, adult daughter of John Robertson and Charlotte Sauteuse, in the presence of Guillaume Fournier and William Shaw (signed), J. N. Ev. de Juliopolis. (page 133)

McIntosh, Marie
        B-686, Marie McIntosh, baptized 1 September 1833 at Fort William, born 17 January 1832, daughter of Donald McIntoche and Charlotte Read, Godfather: Jean Baptiste Deschamps, Godmother: Josephte Hamel, Frs. Boucher priest. (page 114)

McKay, Amable
        B-414, Amable McKay, baptized 7 March 1832, born 11 December 1831, of Amable McKay and Louise Vallee, Godfather: Antoine Pilon, Godmother: Angelique Nolin, J. N. Ev. de Juliopolis priest. (page 59)

McMillan, Helene
        See Jean Baptiste Boyer and Helene McMillan

Mekijiwan, Paul
        B-838, Paul Mekijiwan, baptized 21 August 1834, age 5 years, son of Meyawabittang and Nijikkepinesik, Godmother: Angelique Nolin, G. A. Belcourt priest. (page 139)

Mezinawach, Jean Baptiste
        B-510, Jean Baptiste Mezinawach, Sauteux, baptized 7 December 1832, age about 45 years, Godfather: Jean Roquebrune dit Matiskwiwissens, G. A. Belcourt priest. (page 86)

Mezinawach, Jean Baptiste
        S-37, Jean Baptiste Mezinawach, Sauteux, buried 22 December 1832, age about 45 years, in the presence of Hubert .. and Jean Baptiste Delaunais, G. A. Belcourt priest. (page 86)

Millet, Madeleine
        B-599, Madeleine Millet, baptized 19 January 1830, born in the night, of the legitimate

marriage of Andre Millet, farmer, and Magdeleine Ducharme, Godfather: Alexis Carriere, Godmother: Susanne Ducharme, Fr. Boucher priest. (page 38)

Millet, Marie Domitille
        B-482, Marie Domitille Millet, baptized 10 October 1832, born this morning of the legitimate marriage of Andre Millet and Magdelaine Ducharme, Godfather: Andre Carriere, Godmother: Josephte Ducharme, J. N. Ev. de Juliopolis. (page 77)

Montagnaise, Magdeleine
        B-564, Magdeleine Montagnaise, baptized 6 April 1833, age about 60 years, Godmother: Magdeleine Duboishue dit Berland, G. A. Belcourt priest. (page 96)

Montour, Abraham
        B-493, Abraham Montour, baptized 9 September 1832, born 18 March 1832, of the legitimate marriage of Robert Montour and Marie Spense, Godfather: Andre Beauchemin, Godmother: Isabelle Delaunais, G. A. Belcourt priest. (page 75)

Montour, Sophie
        B-573, Sophie Montour, baptized 3 September 1829, age one month, daughter of Robert Montour, free man, and Sara Spence, Godfather: Jean Baptiste Rivard, Godmother: Marguerite Harrison, Fr. Boucher priest. (page 30)

Montreuille, Alexis
        B-390, Alexis Montreuille, baptized 15 January 1832, born 22 December 1831, of the legitimate marriage of Joseph Montreuille and... (page 48)

Montreuille, Julie
        B-700, Julie Montreuil, baptized 30 October 1833, born yesterday of the legitimate marriage of Joseph Montreuil and Isabelle Botineau, Godfather: Louis Villebrun, Godmother: Louise Collin, C. E. Poire priest. (page 117)

Montreuille, Pierre
        S-48, Pierre Montreuil, buried 13 August 1829, age about sixty years, died yesterday, in the presence of Andre Carriere and Jean MacDonell, Jn. Harper priest. (page 29)

Moran, Paul
        B-568, Paul Moran, baptized 7 August 1829, born 5 August 1829, of Jean Baptiste Moran and Francoise Indian, Godfather: Luc de Repentigny, Godmother: Marie Hool, wife of Paul Larence, Jn Harper priest. (page 29)

Moran, Paul
        S__, Paul Moran, buried 11 September 1829, died yesterday, son of Jean Baptiste Moran

and Francoise Indian, in the presence of Paul Larente and Antoine Caron, Fr. Boucher priest. (page 31)

Morand, Jean Baptiste

B-851, Jean Baptiste Morand, baptized 30 August 1834, born 28 August 1834, of the legitimate marriage of Jean Baptiste Morand and Marie Dubois, Godfather: Michel Monet, Godmother: Angelique Lariviere, J. B. Thibault priest. (page 143)

Morand, Louise: See Francois Saint-Germain and Louise Morand

Moray, Antoine

B-574, Antoine Moray, baptized 6 September 1829, born today, of the legitimate marriage of Francois Moray, farmer, and Marie Larock, Godfather: Joseph Quintal, Godmother: Francoise, wife of Joseph Quintal, Fr. Boucher priest. (page 30)

Morin, Emelie

B-481, Emelie Morin, baptized 29 September 1832, born yesterday morning of the legitimate marriage of Jean Baptiste Morin and Marie Charon, Godfather: Dominique Charon, Godmother: Josephte Severight, J. N. Ev de Juliopolis. (page 77)

Morin, Jean Baptiste

B-892, Jean Baptiste Morin, baptized 21 November 1834, born this morning of the legitimate marriage of Antoine Morin and Therese Roc, Godfather: Jean Baptiste Morin, Godmother: Francoise Piche, J. B. Thibault priest. (page 155)

Morin, Jean Baptiste

B-82, Jean Baptiste Morin, baptized 22 July 1825, born yesterday of the legitimate marriage of Jean Baptiste Morin and Marie Charon dite [Ducharme], Godfather: Charles Larence, Godmother: Josephte Marleau, Ths Destroismaisons priest. (page 6)

Morin, Louis Contois dit and Marie Anne Millet dit Beauchemin

M-139, Louis Contois dit Morin, adult son of Etienne Contois dit Morin and Marguerite Sarcy, married 25 November 1834, Marie Anne Millet dit Beauchemin, daughter of Andre Millet dit Beauchemin and Ch[arlotte] Pelletier, in the presence of Etienne Contois dit Morin and Benjamin Millet ... (page 156)

Morin, Xavier

B-582, Xavier Morin, baptized 18 October 1829, age about 4 months, of the legitimate marriage of Francois Morin and Margueritte, Godfather: Jean-Bapiste Latourellle, Godmother: Magdeleine Nolin, Fr. Boucher priest. (page 32)

Morin, [Marie Therese probably] Contois dit

B-482, ..., baptized 19 August 1832, born 9 July last of the legitimate marriage of Antoine Contois dit Morin and Therese Roc, Godfather: Louis Letendre, Godmother: Marie Fortin, F. Boucher priest. (page 72-73)

Morissette, Jean Baptiste

B-554, Jean Baptiste Morissette, baptized 21 June 1829, age nine months, legitimate son of Arsene Morisette and Therese, Godfather: Pierre Larche.. [Larcheveque ?], Godmother: Magdeleine David, J. N. Ev. de Juliopolis priest. (page 25)

Nadeau, Marguerite

S-71, Marguerite Nadeau, buried 28 August 1834, died yesterday, age 5 months, daughter of Joseph Nadeau and Suzanne Bourdon, in the presence of Pierre Carron and Charles Montigny, C. E. Poire priest. (page 142)

Naud, Benjamin

B-450, Benjamin Naud, baptized 24 June 1832, born today of the legitimate marriage of Amable Naud and Josephte Lagimoniere, Godfather: Benjamin Gervais, Godmother: Josephte Lafr.. , F. Boucher priest. (page 68)

Nault, Boniface

B-871, Boniface Nault, baptized 28 September 1834, born this night of the legitimate marriage of Amable Nault and Josephte Lagimoniere, Godfather: Benjamin Lagimoniere, Godmother: Angelique Carrier, J. B. Thibault priest. (page 149)

Nenahabik Marie

B-835, Marie Nenahabik, baptized 21 August 1834, age 6 years, daughter of Kekijiwe and Nanjadjin, Godmother: Angelique Nolin, G. A. Belcourt priest. (page 139)

Nindinda, Susanne

B-579, Susanne Nindinda (Sauteuse), baptized 13 April 1833, age 14 years, daughter of Nindinda and Gewe, Godmother: Susanne Lorain, G. A. Belcourt priest. (page 98)

Nindinda, [Susanne]

S__, .. baptized 15 April 1833, age 14 years, daughter of Nindinda and Gewe, in the presence of Antoine Desjarlais and Pierre Laroque, G. A. Belcourt priest. (page 98-99)

Nolin, Francois

B-485, Francois Nolin, baptized 21 August 1832, born yesterday of the legitimate marriage of Sieur Augustine Nolin and Dame Helene Cameron, Godmother: Genevieve Nolin, F. Boucher priest. (page 73)

Nolin, Jean-Baptiste

S-25, Jean-Baptiste Nolin, buried 23 January 1832, age about 3 months, son of Jean-Baptiste Normand and Louise Carriere, in the presence of Joseph Baudouin and Pierre Saint-Germain, F. Boucher priest. (page 50)

Nolin, Marie

B-558, Marie Nolin, baptized 5 July 1829, born 7 December 1828, of the legitimate marriage of Sieur Augustin Nolin, tradesman, and Helene Cameron, Godfather: Thomas Harrison, Godmother: Anglique Nolin, who could not sign, the father was absent. Jn. Harper priest. (page 26)

Nolin, Norbert Jean Baptiste

B-84, Norbert Jean Baptiste Nolin, baptized 24 July 1825, by the Bishop of Juliopolis [Joseph-Norbert Provencher] who was also the Godfather, born 26 June last, of the legitimate marriage of Augustin Nolin (signed), trader from Pembina, and Dame Helene Cameron (signed), Godmother: Anna Henriette Tait, wife of Francois Dore, J. N. Ev de Juliopolis. (page 6)

Normand, Michel and Francoise Belanger

M-18, Michel Normand, adult son of the late Jean Baptiste Normand and the deceased Francoise St.Amand, of Vaudreuil District of Montreal, married 4 July 1825, Francoise Belanger, adult daughter of Andre Belanger and a Montagnaise, in the presence of Jean Baptiste Rivard and Francois Dore, Ths Destroismaisons priest. (page 5)

Nouvion, Marie Anne

B-123, Marie Anne Nouvion, baptized 2 October 1825, born 20 March 1821, of Lo... [Louis] Nouvion and Marie Anne Lavalle, Godfather: Pierre Laroc, Godmother: Reine Lagimoniere, Jn Harper. (page 14)

Ojinini, Marguerite

B-455, Marguerite Ojinini, baptized 3 July 1832, daughter of Ojinini Sauteuse and Okijiabons Sauteuse, Godfather: William Shaw, Godmother: Marguerite Savoyard, G. A. Belcourt priest. (page 69)

Ouellette, Francois

B-483, Francois Oilette, baptized 11 August 1832, born 7 August 1832, of Joseph Oilette and Therese Houle, Godfather: Louis Landry, Godmother: Francoise Houle, G. A. Belcourt priest. (page 73)

Ouellette, Isidore

B-632, Isidore Ouellet, baptized 3 April 1830, born yesterday of the legitimate marriage of Joseph Ouellet and Therese Houle, Godmother: Suzanne Bonneau, J. Harper priest. (page 46)

Ouellette, Joseph

B-383, Joseph Oilette, baptized 10 January 1832, born 6 January 1832, of Jaques Oilette and Marie [Marcellais], Godfather: Jean Baptiste Wilky, Godmother: Amable Azure, G. A. Belcourt priest. (page 47)

Ouellette, Pierre

B-559, Pierre Wellet, baptized 5 July 1829, age about 4 months, son of Jacques Wellet and Marie Marcelet, Godfather: Dominique Ducharme, Godmother: Marie Marcelet, Jn. Harper priest. (page 26)

Page, Firmin

B-562, Firmin Page, baptized 11 July 1829, born this morning, of the legitimate marriage of Joseph Page and Agathe Letendre, Godfather: Francois Bruneau (signed), Godmother: Helene McMillan, J. N. Ev. de Juliopolis priest. (page 27)

Page, Joseph and Marguerite Perrault

M-88, Joseph Page, adult son of Joseph Page and Marguerite Poitras, the father and mother of this mission, married 8 June 1829, Marguerite Perrault, minor daughter of Francois Perrault and the deceased Marie Grant, the father and mother, in the presence of Joseph Page, the father of the groom, and Pierre Falcon uncle of the bride, Jn. Harper priest. (page 24)

Page, Joseph

B-385, Joseph Page, baptized 13 January 1832, born day before yesterday of Joseph Page and Marguerite Morin, Godfather: Henry Poitras, Godmother: Marie George, G. A. Belcourt priest. (page 47)

Page, Marguerite

B-633, Marguerite Page, baptized 9 April 1830, born the same day of the legitimate marriage of Joseph Page and Marguerite Morin, Godfather: Pierre Falcon, Godmother: Marie Grant, Jn Harper priest. (page 46)

Paquet, Adelaide

B-__, Adelaide Paquet, baptized 22 June 1825, born yesterday of the legitmate marriage of Antoine Paquet (signed), carpenter, and Augustine Marchand, Godfather: Antoine Boin (signed), Godmother: Justine Marchand (signed Gustine Bion), Jn Harper priest. (page 3)

Paquin, Joseph

B-578, Joseph Paquin, baptized 14 April 1833, age 26 days, son of Joseph Paquin and Marie Lapointe, Godfather: Joseph Desmarais, Godmother: Marie Peltier, F. Boucher priest. (page 98)

St.Boniface Register 1825-1834 (Saved From The Fire)

Parenteau, Adelaide
See Louis Smith and Adelaide Parenteau

Parenteau, Francoise
B-478, Francoise Parenteau, baptized 24 September 1832, born this morning of the legitimate marriage of Pierre Parenteau and Josephte Lorin, Godfather: Jean Parenteau, Godmother: Francoise, J. N. Ev de Juliopolis. (page 76)

Parenteau, Magdeleine
B-636, Magdeleine Parenteau, baptized 22 August 1833, of the legitimate marriage of Joseph Parenteau and Susanne Dagneau, Godfather: Louis de Laronde (signed), Godmother: Magdelaine Dubois, J. N. Ev de Juliopolis. (page 106)

Parenteau, Marie
S-__, Marie [Parenteau], buried 13 October 1832, died -, age 5 years, daughter of Pierre Parenteau, in the presence of Alexandre __. (page 77)

Parenteau, Pierre
B-850, Pierre Parenteau, baptized 29 August 1834, born today of the legitimate marriage of Pierre Parenteau and Josephte Laurin, Godfather: Antoine Dupuis, Godmother: Francoise Laurin, J. B. Thibault priest. (page 143)

Parisien, Angelique
B-596, Angelique Parisien, baptized 6 June 1833, age 22 years, daughter of Jean Baptiste Parisien and Louise, Godmother: Josephte Montagnaze [?], G. A. Belcourt priest. (page 103)

Parisien, Angelique
See Gonzague Zace and Angelique Parisien

Parisien, Bonaventure Leger dit and Marguerite Sauteuse
M-__, Bonaventure Leger dit Parisien, adult son of the deceased Bonaventure Leger dit Parisien and a Sautuese, married 16 June 1834, Marguerite Sauteuse, in the presence of Monsieur Thibault (signed) and Jean Baptiste Dubois, C. E. Poire priest. (page 130)

Parisien, Bonaventure Leger dit
B-795, Bonaventure Leger dit Parisien, baptized 16 June 1834, age 26 years, son of Bonaventure Leger dit Parisien and a Sauteuse, Godfather: Jean Baptiste Dubois, C. E. Poire priest. (page 129)

Parisien, Catherine
B-813, Catherine Parisien, baptized 13 July 1834, daughter of [Jean Baptiste Parisien] and Louise Forcier, Godfather: Amable Delorme, Godmother: Josephte Dion, J. B. Thibault priest.

St.Boniface Register 1825-1834 (Saved From The Fire)

(page 133-134)

Parisien, Catherine
        B-671, Catherine Parisien, baptized 13 October 1833, born 2 October 1833, of Bonaventure Parisien and a Sauteuse, Godfather: Louis Levasseur, Godmother: Catherine Nolin, J. B. Thibault priest. (page 110)

Parisien, Euphrosine
        B-814, Euphrosine Parisien, baptized 13 July 1834, age 7 years, daughter of Jean Baptiste Parisien and Louise Forcier, Godfather: Joseph Ritchot, Godmother: Louise Jerome, J. B. Thibault priest. (page 134)

Parisien, Francois
        B-550, Francois Parisien, baptized 11 July 1829, born 13 September 1828, of Bonaventure Parisien and a Sauteuse, Godfather: Antoine __, Godmother: Marguerite Nolin, J. N. Ev. de Juliopolis. (page 24)

Parisien, Genevieve
        B-888, Genevieve Parisien, baptized 9 November 1834, age 15 days, daughter of Jean Baptiste Parisien and Charlotte Nolin, Godfather: William Shaw (signed), Godmother: Marguerite Sauteuse, J. B. Thibault priest. (page 154)

Parisien, Jean Baptiste
        B-582, Jean Baptiste Parisien, baptized 18 October 1829, born 15 April 1829, of the legitimate marriage of Jean Baptiste Parisien, free man and Charlotte Nolin, Godfather: Jean Baptiste Latourel, Godmother: Helene Cameron, Fr. Boucher priest. (page 32)

Parisien, Leonard or Leonora
        B-812, Leonard [or Leonora], baptized 13 July 1834, age 2 years, daughter of Jean Baptiste Parisien and Louise Forcier, Godfather: Joseph Lafournaise, Godmother: Josephte Delorme, J. B. Thibault priest. (page 133)

Parisien, Magdeleine
        B-393, Magdeleine Parisien, baptized 15 January 1832, born 9 January 1832, before the legitimate marriage of Bonaventure Parisien and Marguerite, Godfather: Louis Vasseur, Godmother: Magdeleine Nolin, F. Boucher priest. (page 49)

Parisien, Magdeleine
        B-495, Magdeleine Parisien, baptized 16 September 1832, born 9 September 1832, of the legitimate marriage of Jean Baptiste Parisien and Charlotte Nolin, Godfather: Antoine Villebrun, Godmother: Susanne Nolin, Boucher priest. (page 75)

Patenaude, Michel

B-488, Michel Patenaude, baptized 21 October 1832, born 16 October 1832, of Michel Patenadue and Marguerite ..., Godfather: Charle Ferdinand Chelly, Godmother: Madeleine .., J. N. Ev. de Juliopolis. (page 79)

Paul, Francoise

B-574, Francoise Paul, baptized 6 April 1833, age 15 years, daughter of Paul Paul and Marguerite Lavallee, Godmother: Marguerite Dease, G. A. Belcourt priest. (page 98)

Paul, Francoise

S-46, Francoise Paul, buried 16 August 1833, age [9 ?] years, of Francois Xavier, White Horse Plains, daughter of Francois Paul and Marguerite Grant, in the presence of Cuthbert Grant and Antoine Lafreniere, C. E. Poire priest. (page 106)

Paul, Jean Baptise and Angelique Godin

M-62, Jean Baptiste Paul (publication at St.Francois Xavier, White Horse Plains), adult son of Joseph Paul and Louise of the Sauteuse tribe, married 29 February 1832, Angelique Godin, adult daughter of Querry Godin and Susanne of the Sioux tribe, in the presence of Olivier Rocquebrune and Michel Richard, G. A. Belcourt priest. (page 55)

Paul, Jean Baptiste

B-407, Jean Baptiste Paul, baptized 28 February 1832, age 36, son of Joseph Paul and Louise, Godfather: Francois Fagnand, F. Boucher priest. (page 53)

Paul, Jean Baptiste, Catherine and Magdeleine

B-575, 576, 577, Jean Baptiste, age 5 years, Catherine, age about 4 years, Magdeleine, age 2 years, baptized 6 September 1829, of Jean Baptiste Paul, free man, and Angelique Piche, Jean Baptiste, Godfather: Joseph Guilbeau, Godmother: Magdeleine Morin, Catherines, Godfather: Louis Gariepy, Godmother: Julie de Rocheblave, Magdeleine, Godfather: Donald McGillis, Godmother: Louise __, the father was absent. Jn. Harper priest. (page 30)

Paul, Jean Baptiste

S-40, Jean Baptiste Paul, buried 24 February 1833, age 11 years, son of Paul Paul and Marguerite Lavallee, in the presence of Louis Lamirande and Jean Baptiste Wilky, F. Boucher priest. (page 93)

Paul, Olivier

B-567, Olivier Paul, baptized 6 April 1833, age 17 years, son of Paul Paul and Marguerite Lavallee, Godfather: William Shaw (signed), J. A. Belcourt priest. (page 97)

Paul, Paul and Marguerite Lavallee

M-74, Paul Paul, adult son of the deceased Paul Paul and the deceased Francoise Joinville, of the parish of Sorel, married 21 May 1832, Marguerite Lavallee, adult daughter of Ignace Lavallee and Josephte Crie, in the presence of Antoine Pilon and Guillaume Rocheleau, F. Boucher priest. (page 65)

Paul, Paul
    S-30, Paul Paul, buried 28 May 1832, died yesterday, son of Paul Paul and Marguerite Lavallee, age 7 years, in the presence of Paul Paul, his father, and Louis Godon, J. N. Ev. de Juliopolis priest. (page 66)

Paul, Pierre
    B-696, Pierre Paul, baptized 20 September 1833, born yesterday, of the legitimate marriage of Jean Baptiste Paul and Angelique Godin, Godfather: Olivier Rocbrune, Godmother: Suzane Sioux, G. A. Belcourt priest (page 116)

Pelletier, Charlotte
    B-557, Charlotte Pelletier, baptized 21 March 1833, born 3 January 1833, of the legitimate marriage of Pierre Pelletier and Agathe Azure, Godfather: Benjamin Lagimoniere, Godmother: Marie Anne Beauchemin, C. E. Poire priest. (page 95)

Pelletier, Lina
    B-632, Lina Pelletier, baptized 5 August 1833, born 23 July 1833, legitimate daughter of Joseph Pelletier and Genevieve Sauteuse, Godfather: Pierre Pangman, Godmother: Marguerite Sauteuse, C. E. Poire priest. (page 105)

Pelletier, Pierre
    B-552, Pierre Pelletier, baptized 21 June 1829, born 18 March 1829, legitimate son of Charles Pelletier and Susanne Bercier, Godfather: Pierre Parenteau, Godmother: Charlotte Pelletier, J. N. Ev. de Juliopolis. (page 25)

Pelletier, Therese
    B-693, Therese Pelletier, baptized 15 October 1833, born yesterday of the legitimate marriage of Charles Pelletier and Susanne Bercier, Godfather: Jean Baptiste Bercier, Godmother: Josephte Bercier, C. E. Poire priest. (page 115)

Pepin, Etienne
    B-473, 11 August 1832, baptized Etienne, age 2 months, illegitimate son of Antoine Pepin and Marie Amelin, Godfather: Jean Yanche, Godmother: Isabelle McDonald, G. A. Belcourt priest.. (page 71)

Perrault, Marguerite
    See Joseph Page and Marguerite Perrault

Petit, Angelique

     B-552, Angelique Petit, baptized 10 March 1833, age 13 years, daughter of Thomas Petit and Marguerite Danis, Godmother: Marguerite, wife of Jean De laderoute, C. E. Poire priest. (page 94)

Petit, Louis

     B-551, Louis Petit, baptized 10 March 1833, age 11 years, son of Thomas Petit and Marguerite Danis, Godfather: Guillaume Rocheleau, C. E. Poire priest. (page 94)

Petitclerc, Jean Baptiste

     B-854, Jean Baptiste Petitclerc, baptized 6 August 1834, born yesterday of the legitimate marriage of Joseph Petitclerc and Therese Hupe, Godmother: Francoise .., J. B. Thibault priest. (page 144)

Petitclerc, Joseph

     B-398, Joseph Petit-Clerc, baptized 16 February 1832, born yesterday of the legitimate marriage of Joseph Petit-Clerc and Therese Huppe, Godfather: Jean Baptiste Cardinal, Godmother: Archange Marcelet, F. Boucher priest. (page 51)

Philippe, Jean Baptiste

     B-139, Jean Baptiste Philippe, baptized 27 October 1825, born today of the legitimate marriage of Jacques Philippe, resident of this mission, and Marguerite Jolicoeur, Godfather: Jean Baptiste Roquebrune, Godmother: Genevieve Lafrance, Ths. Destroismaisons priest. (page 18)

Piche, Joseph and Suzanne Sioux

     M-100, Joseph Piche, resident, adult son of Francois Piche and the deceased Angelique Paul, the father and mother of Saint Ours, District of Montreal, married 8 February 1830, [Suzanne] of the nation of Sioux, in the presence of Joseph Guilbeau and Jean Baptiste Fagnan, Jn Harper priest. (page 40-41)

Piche, Louis

     B-424, Louis Piche, baptized 22 April 1832, born before the legitimate marriage of Josephte Picher and Suzanne Sioux, age 21 years, Godfather: Donald McGillis, G. A. Belcourt priest. (page 61)

Picher, Francoise

     B-426, Francoise Picher, baptized 22 April 1832, age 15 years, daughter of Joseph Picher and Susanne, Godmother: Susanne Bonneau, G. A. Belcourt priest., F. Boucher priest. (page 61)

Picher, Francoise

     See Amable Branconier and Francoise Picher

Picher, Louis and Charlotte Dauphine
M-71, Louis Picher, adult son of Joseph Picher and Suzanne, of the mission of White Horse Plains, married 14 May 1832, Charlotte Dauphine, adult daughter of Michel Dauphine and Victoire Wellet of this mission, in the presence of Olivier Roquebrune and Francois Lionais, G. A. Belcourt priest. (page 63)

Picher, Magdeleine
B-403, Magdeleine Picher, baptized 5 February 1832, age 25 years, daughter of Joseph Picher and Susanne Sioux, Godmother: Josephte Ducharme, G. A. Belcourt priest. (page 52)

Picher, Magdeleine
See Olivier Rochebrune and Magdeleine Picher

Pieds noirs, Magdeleine
See Bazile Bellenger and Magdeleine Pied noirs

Pilon, Antoine and Angelique Lemai
M-68, Antoine Pilon, adult son of Pierre Pilon and Francoise Robidou, married 6 March 1832, Angelique Lemai, adult daughter of Joseph Lemai and Louise Montagnaise. (page 58)

Pilon, Jean Baptiste
B-504, Jean Baptiste Pilon, baptized 9 December 1832, born today of the legitimate marriage of Antoine Pilon and Angelique Lemai, Godfather: Guillaume Rocheleau, Godmother: Francoise St.Germain, G. A. Belcourt priest. (page 83)

Pilon, Jean Baptiste
S-67, Jean Baptiste Pilon, baptized 22 August 1834, age 20 months, son of Antoine Pilon and Angelique Lemai, in the presence of Isidore Bernier and Louis Bousquet, C. E. Poire priest. (page 140)

Plante, Magloire
B-555, Magloire Plante, baptized 26 June 1829, born 24 June 1829, of the legitimate marriage of Basile Plante and Genevieve Gina [Gélinas] dite Lacourse, Godfather: Francois Bruneau (signed), Godmother: Marguerite Harrison, Jn. Harper priest. (page 25)

Plourde, Francois and Suzanne Dubois
M-92, Francois Plourde, adult son of the late Joseph Plourde and the deceased Ursule Arbour, the father and mother from the District of Gaspe, married 3 November 1829, Suzanne Dubois, adult daughter of Francois Dubois and Angelique Lariviere, of this mission, in the presence of Francois Dubois and Jacques Goulet, Jn Harper priest. (page 34)

Plourde, Francois
        B-124, Francois Plourde, baptized 2 October 1825, born yesterday, of Francois Plourde, resident of this mission, and Suzanne Dubois, Godfather: Jeremie Leduc, Godmother: Marie Clavel, Jn. Harper.

Plourde, Olivier
        B-827, Olivier Plourde, baptized 10 August 1834, born this night of the legitimate marriage of Francois Plourde and Susanne Dubois, Godfather: P. Paul, Godmother: Francoise Paul, J. B. Thibault priest. (page 136)

Poitras, Magdeleine
        See Charles Gladu and Magdeleine Potras

Poitras, Pierre and Marie Bruyere
        M-83, Pierre Potras, adult son of the late Andre Potras and Marguerite Grant, married 27 November 1832, Marie Bruyere, minor daughter of Jean Baptiste Bruyere and Francoise, in the presence of Andre Monet and Charles Peltier, F. Boucher priest. (page 84)

Poitras, Sophie and Barthelmi
        B-681, baptized 27 October 1833, Sophie Poitra, age three years about Christmas, Barthelemi Poitra, born three years ago at Christmas, Children of Barthelemi Poitra and Elizabeth Maskegone, Godfather of Sophie: Alexander Wenzsel, Godmother: Catherine Gagnon, Godfather of Barthelemi: Louis Larrivee, Godmother: Marie Crebassa, J. N. Ev de Juliopolis. (page 112)

Pontbriand, Jean Baptiste Boniface
        B-600, Jean Baptiste Boniface Pont Briand, baptized 29 January 1830, born in the night, of the legitimate marriage of Jean-Baptiste Pont Briand and Isabelle Rivard, Godfather: Francois Bruneau (signed), Godmother: Marianne Rivard, Fr. Boucher. (page 38)

Pontbriand, Moyse
        B-440, Moyse Pont Briand, baptized 4 June 1832, born 2 June 1832, of the legitimate marriage of Jean-Baptiste de Pont-Briand and Isabelle Rivard, Godfather: Luc de Repentigny, Godmother: Catherine Boucher, F. Boucher priest. (page 66)

Pontbriand, Suzanne
        B-824, Suzanne de Pontbriand, baptized 5 August 1834, born yesterday of the legitimate marriage of Jean Baptiste de Pontbriand and Isabelle Rivard, Godfather: Gilbert Berio, Godmother: Suzanne Blondeau, J. B. Thibault priest. (page 136)

Pritchard, Joseph
        B-852, Joseph Pritchard, baptized 1 September 1834, born this night of the legitimate marriage of Joseph Pritchard and Louise Parenteau, Godfather: Pierre Parenteau, Godmother:

Emilie Parenteau, J. B. Thibault priest. (page 143)

Racette, Angelique

B-615, Angelique Racette, baptized [between 21 February and 22 February 1830, daughter of Charles Racette and Josephte Sauteuse, Godmother: Josephte Dase, Frs. Boucher priest. (page 43)

Racette, Angelique

See Joseph Adam and Angelique Racette

Racette, Charles and Reine Boucher

M-103, Charles Racette, adult son of Charles Racette and the deceased Josephte Sauteuse, married 15 February 1830, Reine Boucher, minor daughter of Paul Boucher and Francois Saint-Germain, in the presence of Benjamin Marchand and Paul Boucher, Frs. Boucher priest. (page 42)

Racette, Charles

B-612, Charles Racette, baptized 13 February 1830, age 26 years, son of Charles Racette and a female Indian, Godfather: Michel Monet, Jn. Harper priest. (page 41)

Racette, George and Francoise Guilbeau

M-89, George Racette, resident of this colony, adult son of Charles Racette and the deceased Josephte Sauteuse, married 6 July 1829, Francoise Guilbeau, adult daughter of the late Pierre Guilbeau and Angelique Saulteuse, in the presence of Jean Baptiste Rivard and Pierre Guiboche, J. N. Ev. de Juliopolis priest. (page 27)

Racette, George

B-560, George Racette, baptized 5 July 1829 w/o condition, age 22 years, daughter of Charles Racette and Francoise Sauteuse, Godfather: Jean Yanche, J. N. Ev. de Juliopolis priest. (page 26)

Racette, Isabelle

B-809, Isabelle Racette, baptized 10 July 1834, b. this morning of the legitimate marriage of [George Racette] and Francois Guilbeau, Godfather: ..., Godmother: ... La.... (page 132)

Rèche, Susanne

B-128, Susanne Rèche, baptized 12 October 1825, born 2- July 1825, of the legitimate marriage of Joseph Rèche and Susanne Grant, Godfather: Augustin Nolin (signed), Godmother: Helene Cameron, J. N. ev. de Juliopolis. (page 15)

Richard, Julie

B-421, Julie Richard, baptized 13 April 1832, born in the night of the legitimate marriage of Michel Richard and Isabelle Collin, Godfather: Francois Delorme, Godmother: Lousie Moran,

F. Boucher priest. (page 60)

Richard, Michel and Isabelle Collin
    M-61, Michel Richard, adult son of Baptiste Richard and Josephte of the Masquegone tribe, (publication at St.Francois Xavier of White Horse Plains) married 29 February 1832, Isabelle Collin, adult daughter of Antoine Collin and Louise of the Serpente tribe, in the presence of Olivier Rocquebrune and Ambroise Alard, G. A. Belcourt priest. (page 55)

Richard, Michel
    B-405, Michel Richard, baptized 28 February 1832, age 38 years, son of Jean Baptiste Richard and Josephte, Godfather: Charles Gladus, F. Boucher priest. (page 53)

Ritchot, Andre
    B-569, Andre Ritchot, baptized 8 August 1829, born yesterday of the legitimate marriage of Joseph Ritchot and Josephte Maillou, Godfather: Andre Carriere, Godmother: Marie Morin, Jn. Harper priest. (page 29)

Ritchot, Joseph and Josephte Maillou
    M-27, Joseph Ritchot, adult son of the deceased Michel Ritchot and the deceased Marguerite Crevier, of the parish of St.Michel of Yamaska, married 17 October 1825, Josephte Maillou, daughter of Antoine Maillou and a Sarcie, in the presence of Thimothee Dionne and Victor Chenier, J. N. Ev de Juliopolis. (page 17)

Ritchot, Joseph
    B-136, Joseph Ritchot, baptized 16 October 1825, age 13 years, son of Joseph Ritchot and Jos. Maillou, Godfather: Francois Charon, J. N. Ev de Juliopolis. (page 16)

Ritchot, Marie
    B-449, Marie Ritchot, baptized 11 June 1832, born yesterday of the legitimate marriage of Joseph Ritchot and Josephte Mailloux, Godfather: Jean Baptiste Mor.., Godmother: Marguerite Nolin, F. Boucher priest. (page 68)

Rivard, Marie Anne
    See Andre Carriere and Marie Anne Rivard

Rivets, Louise
    See Augustin Mainville

Robertson, Charlotte
    B-810, Charlotte Robertson, baptized 11 July 1834, age 35 years, daughter of John Robertson and Charlotte Sauteuse, Godmother: Marguerite Nolin, J. B. Thibault priest. (page 133)

St.Boniface Register 1825-1834 (Saved From The Fire)

Robertson, Charlotte
        See John McIntosh and Charlotte Robertson

Robillard, Andre
        B-578, Andre Robillard, baptized 18 September 1829, born 22 August 1828, of the legitimate marriage of Jean Baptiste Robillard, free man, and Marie Rose Lagimoniere, Godfather: Francois Charon, Godmother: Magdeleine David, Fr. Boucher priest. (page 31)

Robillard, Marguerite
        B-472, Marguerite Robillard, baptized 4 August 1832, born today of the legitimate marriage of Jean Baptiste Robillard and Rose Antoinette Lagimoniere, Godfather: Prospere Choret, Godmother: Angelique Plante, G. A. Belcourt priest. (page 71)

Roc, Joseph
        B-422, Joseph Roc, baptized 21 April 1832, born before the legitimate marriage of Joseph Roc and anAssiniboine, Godfather: William [?]. F. Boucher priest. (page 60)

Rocbrune, Antoine and Marie Genton dit Daupine
        M-134, Antoine Rocbrune, adult son of Jean Baptiste Rocbrune and Louise Sautuese, married 15 September 1834, Marie Genton dit Dauphine, daughter of Michel Genton dit Dauphine and Victoire Ouellet, in the presence of Jean Baptiste Rocbrune and ... Genton dit Daupine, J. B. Thibault priest. (page 145)

Rocbrune, Charles
        B-664, Charles Rocbrune, baptized 15 September 1833, born yesterday of the legitimate marriage of Jean Baptiste Rocbrune and Josephte Charron [?], Godfather: Louis Marsant, Godmother: Therese Belanger, J. N. Ev de Juliopolis. (page 108)

Rocbrune, Francois
        B-811, Francoise Rocbrune, baptized 12 July 1834, born this morning of the legitimate marriage of Antoine Rocbrune and Francoise Laliberte, Godfather: Alexis Goulet, Godmother: Marie Macon, J. B. Thibault priest. (page 133)

Rocbrune, Joseph
        B-479, Joseph Roquebrune, baptized 23 September 1832, born 15 September 1832, of the legitimate marriage of Olivier Roquebrune and Maglelaine Picher, Godfather: Joseph Guilbeau, Godmother: Charlotte Dauphinais, G. A. Belcourt priest. (page 77)

Rocbrune, Louis and Marie
        B-93 and B-94, Louis and Marie Rocbrune, baptized 7 August 1825, Louis, born 16 July 1823, Marie, born 4 March 1821, of Olivier Rocbrune and Magdelaine Piche, Godparents for Louis: Jean Baptiste Boucher and Marguerite Rocbrune, Godparents for Marie: Jean Baptiste

Rocbrune and Genevieve L..., Jn Harper priest. (page 7)

Rocheblave, Julie
        B-112, Julie Rocheblave, baptized 24 September 1825, without condition, age 18 years, daughter of Pierre de Rocheblave Esquire and Marguerite Boucher, Godmother: Angelique St.Germain, Ths. Destroismaisons priest. (page 11)

Rocheblave, Julie
        See Donald McGillis and Julie Rocheblave

Rocheblave, Julie
        See Jean Baptiste Boucher and Julie de Rocheblave

Rocheblave, Marie de
        S-7, Marie de Rocheblave, buried 18 August 1825, died day before yesterday, age about 24, in the presence of Jean Baptiste Boucher and Benjamin Marchand, Ths Destroismaisons priest. (page 9)

Rocheblave, Marie
        See Jean Baptiste Lafontaine and Marie de Rocheblave

Rochebrune, Olivier and Magdeleine Picher
        M-58, Olivier Roque-Brune, adult son of Jean Baptiste Roquebrune and the deceased Marguerite Jolicoeur, the father and mother of the parish of Rigaud, married 6 February 1832, (after publications at the parish of St. Francois-Xavier of White Horse Plains) Magdeleine Picher, adult daughter of Joseph Picher and Susanne of the Sioux tribe, in the presence of Francois Gariepy and Pierre Divertissant, G. A. Belcourt priest. (page 53)

Rocheleau, Guillaume and Marie Adam
        M-67, Guillaume Rocheleau, adult son of the deceased Guillaume Rocheleu and Amable Taillefer, of Montreal, married 6 March 1832, Marie Adam, adult daughter of Jean Baptiste Adam and Louise Quebec, in the presence of Antoine Ca.. and Jacques Cardinal, G. A. Belcourt priest. (page 58)

Rocheleau, Marie
        B-497, Marie Rocheleau, baptized 21 November 1832, born this morning of the legitimate marriage of Guillaume Rocheleau and Marie Adam, Godfather: Antoine Pilon, Godmother: Marguerite Dease (signed), J. N. Ev. de Juliopolis. (page 81)

Rocque, Joseph
        B-402, Joseph Rocque, baptized 21 February 1832, age about 50 years, son of Joseph Rocque and a Sioux, Godfather: Gaspard Brousse, Frs. Boucher priest. (page 52)

Rondeau, Marguerite
       B-703, Marguerite Rondeau, baptized 19 November 1833, born today of the legitimate marriage of Joseph Rondeau and Joseph[te] Beaulieu, Godfather: Guillaume .., Godmother: Marguerite, G. A. Belcourt priest. (page 118)

Ross, John
       B-493, John Ross, baptized 28 October 1832, born 21 October 1832, of Hughes Ross and Saly Short of White Horse Plains, Godfather: Louis Gariepi, Godmother: Marguerite ..., G. A. Belcourt priest. (page 80)

Roussile, Angele
       See Augustin Mainville

Roy, Francois
       B-566, Francois Roy, baptized [6 April 1833], age 18 years, son of Francois Roy and Marie Collin, Godfather: Joseph Nolin, G. A. Belcourt priest. (page 97)

Sahys, Francoise
       B-487, Francoise Sahys, baptized 21 October 1832, born 17 October 1832, of the legitimate marriage of Francois Louis Sahys (signed) and Josephte, Godfather: Antoine Rocbrune, Godmother: Josephte Laliberte, J. N. Ev de Juliopolis. (page 79)

Sarcie, Marguerite
       See Etienne Comtois and Marguerite Sarcie

Sarcis, Marie
       B-127, Marie, of the nation of Sarcis, baptized 11 October 1825, age 65 years, Godfather: Joseph Allie, Ths. Destroismaisons priest. (page 15)

Sausteuse, Josephte
       S-886, Josephte Sauteuse, baptized 3 November 1834, age about 40 years, Godmother: Francoise Laurin, J. B. Thibault priest. (page 153)

Sauteuse, Catherine
       S-48, Catherine Wisrapikkahemek [?], Sauteuse, buried 31 August 1833, age about 60 years, ... (page 106)

Sauteuse, Isabelle
       B-565, Isabelle Sauteuse, baptized 6 April 1833, age about .. years. (page 96)

Sauteuse, Marguerite
> B-597, Marguerite of the nation of Sauteuse, baptized 10 January 1830, age about 40 years, Godmother: Josephte Fagnan, Jn Harper Priest. (page 37)

Sauteuse, Marguerite
> B-717, Marguerite Sauteuse, baptized 19 January 1834, age 57 years, Godmother: Angelique Nolin, J. B. Thibault priest. (page 124)

Sauteuse, Marguerite
> B-409, Marguerite Sauteuse, baptized 28 February 1832, age 30 years, woman of Jean Baptiste Gariepy, Godmother: Marguerite Poitras, F. Boucher priest. (page 54)

Sauteuse, Marguerite
> B-796, Marguerite Sauteuse, baptized 16 June 1834, age 20 years, Godmother: Angelique Nolin. (page 129)

Sauteuse, Marguerite
> See Jean Baptiste Gariepy and Marguerite Sauteuse

Sauteuse, Marguerite
> See Pierre George and Marguerite Sauteuse

Sauteuse, Marguerite
> See Louis Boisvert and Marguerite Sauteuse

Sauteuse, Marguerite
> See Bonaventure Leger dit Parisien and Marguerite Sauteuse

Sauteuse, Marie
> B-429, Marie Sauteuse, born __ May 1832. (page 61)

Sauteuse, Marie
> See Antoine Lambert and Marie Sauteuse

Sauteux, Cuthbert
> S-44, Cuthbert, buried 25 May 1833, age 4 years, son of Winakamigowinine and Negane, Sauteux, in the presence of Cuthbert Grant and Louis Gariepy, C. E. Poire priest. (page 103)

Sauteux, Josephte
> B-776, Josephte, baptized 5 May 1834, age one year, daughter of Peccikijik and Josephte Sauteux, Godmother: Angelique Nolin, G. A. Belcourt priest. (page 127)

Sauteux, Louis
        S__, Louis Sauteux, buried 5 July 1834 on the prairie, in the presence of Jean Baptiste Wilky and Joseph Vallee, C. E. Poire priest. (page 137)

Sauteux, Marguerite
        See Angus McGillis and Marguerite Sauteux

Sauteux, unknown
        B-775 .... of Peccikijik and J..., Godmother: Angelique Nolin, G. A. Belcourt priest. (page 127)

Sautuese, Alexis
        B-831, Alexis, baptized 19 July 1834, born 2 April 1834 of parents from the Sautuese tribe, Godfather: Alexis Belgarde, Godmother: Marguerite Lefort, C. E. Poire priest. (page 137)

Sautuese, Josephte
        See Pierre Demers and Josephte Sauteuse

Sautuese, Marie Angelique
        B-109, Marie Angelique Sauteuse, baptized 18 September 1825, age about 60 years, sauteuse of this mission, Godfather: Gaspard Brousse, no Godmother, Ths. Destroismaisons, priest. (page 10)

Sauve, Jean
        B-568, Jean Sauve, baptized 6 April 1833, age 21 years, son of Jean Baptiste Sauve and Marguerite Maskegon, Godfather: Louis Galarneau, G. A. Belcourt priest. (page 97)

Savoyard, Joseph and Marguerite Dubois
        M-121, Joseph Savoyard, adult son of Toussaint Savoyard and Marguerite Sauteuse, married 7 January 1834, Marguerite Dubois, minor daughter of Francois Dubois and Angelique Lariviere, in the presence of Jean Baptiste Wilky and Antoine Vandal, J. B. Thibault priest. (page 123)

Savoyard, Joseph
        B-704, Joseph Savoyard, baptized 20 November 1833, born of the legitimate marriage of Pierre Savoyard and Lo[uise] Dubois, Godfather: Joseph Delorme, Godmother: .. Savoyard, G. A. Belcourt priest. (page 118)

Sayer, Edouard
        B-457, Edouard Serre, baptized 8 July 1832, age 2 years, son of Guillaume Serre and Josephte Frobisher, of White Horse Plains, Godfather: Joseph Piche, Godmother: Marguerite Grant, G. A. Belcourt priest. (page 70)

Sayer, Guillaume
        B-461, Guillaume Serre, baptized 15 July 1832, age 5 years, son of Guillaume Serre ...., Godfather: Louis Gariepe. (page 70)

Sayer, Isidore
        B-484, Isidore Sayer, baptized 16 October 1832, born 4 October 1832, of Guillaume Sayer and Josephte Frobisher, Godfather: Guillaume Rocheleau, Godmother: Marie Fortin, J. N. Ev de Juliopolis. (page 78)

Sayer, Isidore
        S-35, Isidore Sayer, buried 19 October 1832, died yesterday, son of Guillaume Sayer and Josephte Forbisher, in the presence of Moyse Lamere and Gabriel Lafournaise, J. N. Ev. De Juliopolis. (page 79)

Serpent, Francoise
        See Jean Baptiste Briere and Francoise Serpent

Severight, Josephte
        See Alexis Goulet and Josephte Severight
Short, Genevieve
        B-539, Genevieve Short, baptized 17 February 1833, age 25 years, Godmother: Marie, C. E. Poire priest. (page 90)

Short, Genevieve
        See Jean Baptiste Versail and Genevieve Short

Short, James and Charlotte Gladu
        M-84, James Short, adult son of James Short and Betsey Sauteuse, married 27 November 1832, Charlotte Gladu, adult daughter of Charles Gladu and Marguerite Ross, in the presence of Charles Gladu and Louis Gardepy, F. Boucher priest. (page 84-85)

Short, Jamy
        B-501, Jamy Short, baptized 25 November 1832, son of James Short and Betsy Sauteuse, age twenty one years and six months, Godfather: Charles Gladu, G. A. Belcourt priest. (page 82)

Sinclair, Marguerite
        B-791, Marguerite Sinclair, baptized [between 18 May and 1 June 1834, age two years, daughter of Peter Sinclair and Josephte Roy, Godfather: Francois Roy, Godmother: Isabel Lafreniere, J. B. Thibault priest. (page 129)

Sinclair, Marie
    See Augustin Mainville

Sioux, Suzanne
    See Joseph Piche and Suzanne Sioux

Smith, Joseph
    B-556, Joseph Smith, baptized 21 March 1833, born yesterday of the legitimate marriage of Louis Smith and Adelaide Parenteau, Godfather: Joseph Desmarais, Godmother: Marguerite Lafournaise, C. E. Poire priest. (page 95)

Smith, Louis and Adelaide Parenteau
    M-97, Louis Smith, adult son of Sieur Smith and Susanne Le Clerc, the father and mother, married 8 February 1830, Adelaide Parenteau, minor daughter of Joseph Parenteau and the deceased Susanne Cree, in the presence of Joseph Parenteau and Joseph Decoteau, Fr. Boucher priest. (page 39)

Smith, Louis
    B-606, Louis Smith, baptized 7 February 1830, age about 22 years, son of Sr. Smith and Susanne Leclair, Godfather: Andre Millet, Fr. Boucher priest. (page 39)

Soubrero, Judith
    S-6, Judith Soubrero, buried 12 August 1825, died yesterday, age 18 days, [legitimate] daughter of Jean Baptiste Soubrero and Josephte Lalonde, in the presence of Francois Bruneau and Louis Tremblay, Jn Harper priest. (page 8)

Souliere, Basile
    B-579, Basile Souliere, baptized 4 October 1829, born yesterday, of Basile Souliere and Josephte Boisvert, Godfather: Joseph Parenteau, Godmother: Josephte Daze, J. N. Ev. de Juliopolis priest. (page 31)

Souliere, Basile
    S-27, Basile Souliere, buried 28 January 1832, age about 3 years, son of Basile Souliere and Josephte Boisvert, in the presence of Louis Carriere and Pascal Montour, F. Boucher priest. (page 51)

St.Cyr, Jean Baptiste and Marie Cadot
    M-99, Jean Baptiste St.Cyr, adult son of the late Joseph St.Cyr and the deceased Genevieve, his father and mother of Nicolet, Three Rivers District, married 18 February 1833, Marie Cadot, widow of Joseph Dubois, in the presence of Joseph Caplette and Jean Baptiste Versailles, F. Boucher priest. (page 90-91)

St.Boniface Register 1825-1834 (Saved From The Fire)

St.Denis, Martin

B-145, Martin St.Denis, baptized .. December 1825, age 15 days, son of Francois St.Denis, free man, and Sophie Jacklins, Godfather: Martin Jerome, Godmother: Angelique Letendre, Ths Destroismaisons priest. (page 21)

St.Denys, Elie

B-820, Elie St.Denys, baptized 26 July 1834, born this night of the legitimate marriage of Jacques St.Denys and Genevieve Durant, Godfather: Elie Carrier, Godmother: Catherine Morin, J. B. Thibault priest. (page 135)

St.Denys, Elie

S-64, Elie St.Denys, buried 14 August 1834, son of Jaques St.Denys and Genevieve D[urant], in the presence of Andre Carriere and Isidore Bernier, C. E. Poire priest. (page 138)

St.Denys, Jacques and Genevieve Durant

M-75, Jacques St.Denys, adult son of the deceased Jacques St.Denys and Catherine Gervais, the father and mother of the Pointe ..., married 19 June 1832 at Bas de la Riviere Winnipeg, Genevieve Durant, minor daughter of Louis Durant and Josephte Dion, in the presence of Simon McKay, Louis Cam.. [?], Bte. Lornie [?], J. N. Ev. De Juliopolis priest. (page 68)

St.Denys, Lizette

B-619, Lizette Saint-Denys, baptized 28 February 1830, Louise born 13 February 1830, of the legitimate marriage of Francois Saint-Denys and Sophie ..., Godfather: Antoine Dupuys, Godmother: Marguerite Alary, Fr. Boucher priest. (page 44)

St.Denys, Paul

B-441, Paul St.Denys, baptized 8 June 1832, born yesterday, of the legitimate marriage of Paul St.Denys and Catherine Gariepe, Godfather: Louis Gardepe, Godmother: Josephte Ducharme, F. Boucher priest. (page 66)

St.Denys, Pierre

B-434, Pierre Saint-Denys, baptized 13 May 1832, born 8 May 1832, of the legitimate marriage of Francois Saint-Denys and Sophie Laen,Godfather: Francois Vestrou, Godmother: Magdeleine Vivier, F. Boucher priest. (page 64)

St.Germain, Francois and Louise Morand

M-90, Francois Saint-Germain, free man of this mission, adult son of the deceased Andre Lemaire Saint-Germain and Ursule Despres of St-Eustache of the Rivere Duchene, married 21 September 1829, Louise Morand, minor daughter of Jean Baptiste Morand and Francoise Brunoche, in the presence of Jean Baptiste Moran, father of the bride and Pierre Berard, friend of the groom.   (The groom signed)   Francois Boucher priest. (page 31)

St.Boniface Register 1825-1834 (Saved From The Fire)

St.Germain, Francoise
    See Paul Boucher and Francoise St.Germain

St.Germain, Joseph Brissard dit and Marie Cadotte
    M-115, Joseph Brissard dit St.Germain, adult son of Alexis Brissard dit St.Germain and Louise Chabotte of Maskinonge, Lower Canada, married 19 November 1833, Marie Cadotte, adult daughter of Laurent Cadotte and a Maskegone, in the presence of Joseph Descoteau and Joseph Quintal, G. A. Belcourt priest. (page 118)

St.Germain, Josephte
    B-866, Josephte St.Germain, baptized 28 September 1834, age 6 years, daughter of Pierre St.Germain and Louise Alary, Godfather: Antoine Carron, Godmother: Angelique St.Germain, J. B. Thibault priest. (page 148)

St.Germain, Louise
    B-867, Louise St.Germain, baptized 28 September 1834, age one year, daughter of Pierre St.Germain and Louise Alary, Godfather: Pierre St.Germain, Godmother: Catherine Morin, J. B. Thibault priest. (page 148)

St.Germain, Pierre and Louise Henry
    M-138 (2nd), Pierre St.Germain, adult son of the deceased Antoine St.Germain and a Montagnaise, married 17 November 1834, Louise Henry, adult daughter of Sieur Robert Henry and a Montagnaise, in the presence of Antoine Carron and Eustache Carron, J. B. Thibault priest. (page 155)

Taylor, Thomas
    B-451, Thomas Taylor, baptized 16 June 1832, born 25 August 1831 of the legitimate marriage of Thomas Taylor and Marie Keith, Godmother: Francoise Lorin, J. N. ev de Juliopolis priest. (page 68)

Tcikinakoce, Augustin
    B-847, Augustin Tcikinakoce, baptized 28 August 1834, age 4 years, son of Tcikinakoce and Ikkwesens, Godfather: Charles de Montigny (signed), Godmother: Genevieve Nolin, J. B. Thibault priest. (page 142)

Tcikinakoce, Jean Baptiste
    B-848, Jean Baptiste Tcikinakoce, baptized 28 August 1834, age one year, son of Tcikinakoce and Ikkwesens, Godfather: Isidore Bernier (signed), Godmother: Mar[guerite] Davis, J. B. Thibault priest. (page 142)

Tcikinakoce, Marguerite
    B-849, Marguerite [Tcikinakoce], baptized 28 August 1834, age six years, child of

Tciki[nakoce and A'Ikkwesens], Godfather: Pierre Carron (signed), Godmother: Marguerite Davis, J. B. Thibault priest. (page 142-143)

Thomas, Marie

      B-829, Marie Thomas, baptized 10 August 1834, age 2 years, daughter of Joseph Thomas and a Sauteuse, Godfather: Jean Baptiste Charbonneau, Godmother: Isabel Duval, J. B. Thibault priest. (page 137)

Thomas, Marie

      S-77, Marie Thomas, buried 9 October 1834, died yesterday, age 2 years, daughter of Joseph Thomas and a Metisse, in the presence of Louis Bousquet and Pierre Carron, J. B. Thibault priest. (page 151)

Thorne, Genevieve

      B-883, Genevieve Torn, baptized 19 October 1834, age 4 years, daughter of George Torn and Marie Lemure, Godfather: Pierre Roseau dit Beaumet, Godmother: Genevieve Grant, J. B. Thibault priest. (page 152)

Thorne, George

      B-881, George Torn, baptized 19 October 1834, age 5 years, son of George Torn and Marie Lemure, Godfather: Amable Branconnier, Godmother: Isabelle Normand, J. B. Thibault. (page 151)

Thorne, unknown

      B-882, ...Torn, baptized 19 October 1834, age 2 years, [of George Torn and Marie Lemire], Godfather: Peter Heyden, Godmother: Isabelle Normand, J. B. Thibault. (page 151-152)

Tifau, Louis and Isabelle Lionay

      M-56, Louis Tifau, adult son of Bazile Tifau and the deceased Marie, of this mission, married Isabelle Lionay, minor daughter of Franocis Lionay and Louise, in the presence of Bazile Tifau and Francois Lionay, F. Boucher priest. (page 50)

Trottier, Michel

      B-442, Michel Trottier, baptized 8 June 1832, born yesterday, of the legitimate marriage of Andre Trotier and Marguerite Paquette, Godfather: Michel Alard, Godmother: Marie Vestro, ... priest. (page 66)

Turcot, Vital

      B-423, Vital Turcot, baptized 21 April 1832, born before the legitimate marriage of Jean Baptiste Turcot and a Sautuese, Godfather: Charles Belgarde, F. Boucher priest. (page 60)

Turpin, Joseph

B-401, Joseph Turpin, baptized 19 February 1832, born 8 February 1832, of the legitimate marriage of Joseph Turpin and Angelique Laliberte, Godfather: Joseph Hupe, Godmother: Marguerite, F. Boucher priest. (page 52)

Vallee, Louis

B-427, Louis Vallee, baptized 29 April 1832, age 3 days, daughter of Louis Vallee and Louise Martel, Godfather: Louis Carriere, Godmother: Louise Carriere, G. A. Belcourt priest. (page 61)

Vallee, Toussaint

B-494, Toussaint Valle, baptized 8 September 1832, born 8 March, son of Joseph Valle and Louise Page, Godfather: Henri Poitras, Godmother: Marguerite Poitras, F. Boucher priest. (page 75)

Vanasse, Jean Baptiste

B-818, Jean Baptiste Vatnase [Vanasse], baptized 13 July 1834, age 10 months, son of Pierre Vatnase and Julie Parisien, Godfather: Jean Dumont, Godmother: Marguerite. .. (page 134)

Vandal, Jean Baptiste

B-799, Jean Baptiste Vandal, baptized 8 July 1834, age about 2 years, son of Pierre Vandal and Charlotte Hughes, Godfather: Pierre Carron (signed), Godmother: Madeline Desfonts, J. B. Thibault priest. (page 131)

Vandal, Marguerite

B-798, Marguerite Vandal, baptized 8 July 1834, age 5 years, daughter of Pierre Vandal [and Charlotte Hughes], Godmother: Marie Anne Martin, J. B. Thibault priest. (page 130-131)

Vandal, Pierre

B-797, Pierre Vandal, baptized 8 July 1834, age 6 years, son of Pierre Vandal and Charlotte Hughes, Godfather: Charles de Montigny (signed), Godmother: Marguerite Nolin, J. B. Thibault priest. (page 130)

Vandal, Pierre

B-567, Pierre Vandale, baptized 2 August 1829, born 14 July 1829, of the legitimate marriage of Joseph Vandale, free man, and Marie Lachevretiere, Godfather: Pierre Berard, Godmother: Marie Clavassa [Crebassa], Jn. Harper priest. (page 29)

Vandal, Pierre

S-41, Pierre Vandal, buried 1 March 1833, age about 4 years, son of Joseph Vandal and Marie Lachevretiere, in the presence of Toussaint Vaudry and Joseph Defond, G. A. Belcourt priest. (page 93)

St.Boniface Register 1825-1834 (Saved From The Fire)

Vandal, Pierre

S-69, Pierre Vandal, buried 22 August 1834, died this morning, age 6 years, son of Pierre Vandal and Charlotte Hughes, in the presence of Isidore [Bernier] and Louis Bousquet.... (page 140)

Vasseur, Jean Baptiste

B-626, Jean Baptiste Vasseur, baptized 1 April 1830, born night before last, of the legitimate marriage of Louis Vasseur and Marguerite Peltier, Godfather: Pierre Peltier, Mg: Marie Parenteau, F. Boucher priest. (page 45)

Vasseur, Louis

B-129, Louis Vasseur, baptized 13 October 1825, born 24 September 1825, of the legitimate marriage of Louis Vasseur and Marguerite Peltier, Godfather: Antoine Gruet, Godmother: Marguerite Nolin, J. N. Ev de Juliiopolis. (page 15)

Vaudry, Joseph

B-509, Joseph Vaudry, baptized 25 December 1832, age 5 days, legitimate son of Toussaint Vaudry and Marie Anne Crebassa, Godfather: Antoine Dupuis, Godmother: Francoise Lorin, J. N. Ev de Juliopolis. (page 86)

Vaudry, Louise

S-79, Louise Vaudry, buried 24 November 1834, died yesterday, age 4 years, daughter of Toussaint Vaudry and Marie Anne Crebassa, in the presence of Joseph Vandal and Augustin Martineau, J. B. Thibault priest. (page 156)

Venne, Joseph

B-498, Joseph Venne, baptized 21 November 1832, born this morning of the legitimate marriage of Pierre Jean Venne and Marie Charette, Godfather: Benjamin Lajimoniere, Godmother: Rosalie Dujaneau, J. N. Ev de Juliopolis. (page 81)

Vermet, Antoine

B-582, Antoine [Vermet], baptized 29 April 1833, born day before yesterday of the legitimate marriage of [Joseph Vermet] and Angelique Laliberte, Godfather: ... Laliberte, C. E. Poire priest. (page 99-100)

Vermet, Joseph and Angelique Laliberte

M-93, Joseph Vermet, free man of this mission, adult son of the late Joseph Vermet and the deceased Josephte Vilebrune, his mother and father, married 11 January 1830, Angelique Laliberte, minor daughter of Pierre Laliberte and the deceased Josephte Baudry, in the presence of Antoine Legros, friend of the groom, Joseph Laliberte, father of the bride, Frs. Boucher priest. (page 36)

Vermet, Joseph
    B-596, Joseph Vermet, baptized 10 January 1830, about -4 years, son of the late Joseph Vermet and Josephte Vellebrun, Godfather: Joseph Enaud dit Delorme, Frs. Boucher priest. (page 36)

Versailles, Jean Baptiste and Genevieve Short
    M-103, Jean Baptiste Versail, adult son of the late Louis Versail and Magdeleine Montagnaise, married 18 February 1833, Genevieve Short, adult daughter of James Short and Elizabeth Crise, in the presence of Antoine Carron and Pierre Parenteau, F. Boucher priest. (page 92)

Versailles, Jean Baptiste
    B-633, Jean Baptiste Versaille, baptized 5 August 1833, age 15 days, of the legitimate marriage of Jean Baptiste Versaille and Jenny Short, Godfather: Joseph Guilbault, Godmother: Marguerite Sauteuse, C. E. Poire priest. (page 105)

Versailles, Jean Baptiste
    B-541, Jean Baptiste Versaille, baptized 18 February 1833, son of Louis Versaille and a Montagnaise, Godfather: Jean Baptiste Laurence, C. E. Poire priest. (page 90)

Versailles, Louise
    B-586, Louise Versail, baptized 2 November 1829, age about 27 years, daughter of Louis Versail and Magdeleine Montagnaise, Godmother: Josephte Letendre, Francois Boucher pte. (page 33)

Versailles, Louise
    See Jacques Goulet and Louise Versailles

Versailles, Marguerite
    B-666, Marguerite Versaille, baptizcd 20 September 1833, born yesterday of the legitimate marriage of Pierre Versaille and Josephte Letendre, Godfather: Pierre Ducharme, Godmother: Catherine Macon, J. B. Thibault priest. (page 108)

Versailles, Marie
    B-617, Marie Versailles, baptized 24 February 1830, born 22 February 1830, of the legitimate marriage of Pierre Versailles and Josephte Letendre, Godfather: Francois C..., Godmother: Marie Letendre, Jn. Harper priest. (page 44)

Versailles, Pierre and Josephte Letendre
    M-13, Pierre Versailles, adult son of Louis Versailles and Magdelaine Montagnaise, married 6 June 1825, Josephte Letendre, adult daughter of Jean Baptiste Letendre and Josephte Indian, in the presence of Francois Delaunay and Benjamin Marchand, Ths. Destroismaisons

priest. (page 1-2)

Versailles, Pierre

      B-556, Pierre Versaille, baptized 28 June 1829, age 4 days, son of Jean Baptiste Versaille and Jinai [Jenny] Short, Godfather: Jacques Goulet, Godmother: Marie Letendre, J. N. Ev. de Juliopolis, priest. (page 26)

Versailles, Scholastique

      B__, Scholastique Versailles, baptized 16 June 1825, born yesterday of the legitimate marriage of Pierre Versailles and Josephte Letendre, Godfather: Francois Dore, Godmother: Archange Lalonde, Ths. Destroimaissons priest. (page 3)

Villebrun, Antoine and Archange Marsolet

      M-66, Antoine Villebrun, adult son of Louis Villebrun and Marianne of the Collets tribe, married 5 March 1832, Archange Marsolet, minor daughter of Jean Baptiste Marsolet and Angelique Assiniboine, in the presence of Joseph Deganne and Paul Boucher G. A. Belcourt priest. (page 57)

Villebrun, Louis and Louise Collin

      M-30, Louis Villebrun, adult son of Louis Villebrune, resident of this mission, and Marie Anne of the nation of Collets, the father and mother are of this mission, married 21 Nov 1825, Louise Collin, minor daughter of Joseph Collin and Josephte Sauteuse, the father and mother are of this mission, in the presence of Louis Villebrun, father of the groom, and Joseph Delorme, brother-in-law of the bride [groom], Ths. Destroismaisons priest. (page 20)

Villebrun, Louis

      B-143, Louis Villebrun, baptized 20 November 1825, age 24 years, son of Louis Villebrun, resident of this mission, and Marie Anne of the nation of Collets, Godfather: Jean Baptiste Latourelle, Ths Destroismaisons, priest. (page 20)

Villebrun, Louis

      B-551, Louis Villebrun, baptized 14 June 1829, born 11 June 1829, of the legitimate marriage of Louis Villebrun and Louise Colin, Godfather: Benjamin Millet, Godmother: Suzanne Ducharme, Jn Harper priest. (page 24)

Villebrun, Marguerite

      See Francois Desmarais and Marguerite Villebrun

Villebrun, Marie

      B-437, Marie ... baptized 25 May 1832, of the legitimate marriage of Lo... and Louise Collin. (page 65)

St.Boniface Register 1825-1834 (Saved From The Fire)

Villeneuve, Sophie

B-865, Sophie Villeneuve, baptized 28 September 1834, daughter of Michel Velleneuve and ..., Godfather: ... Gaudry, Godmother: Emelie Wenzel, J. B. Thibault priest. (page 147-148)

Vivier, Marguerite

S__, Marguerite Vivier, buried 30 August 1832, died day before yesterday, age ... (page 73)

Vivier, Marguerite

See Michel Desmarais and Marguerite Vivier

Vivier, Marie

See Joseph Descoteaux and Marie Vivier

Vivier, [Marie]

B-492, M... Vivier, baptized 21 October 1832, born 5 October 1832 of Alexis Vivier and __ Short of White Horse Plains, Godfather: Pierre Boyer, Godmother: Francoise Piche, G. A. Belcourt priest. (page 80)

Warchter, Marie Elonire

S-9, Marie Elonire Warchter, buried 11 Dec 1825, died yesterday, daughter of Christian Warchter and Marie Clavelle, in the presence of Jean Baptiste Laderoute and Jean Baptiste Chaurette, Ths. Destroismaisons priest. (page 21)

Wells, B.

M-107, .. B. Wells, .. son of Joseph Wells and ..., married 28 May 1833, ... (page 104)

Wentzel, Emilie

B-701, Emilie Wentzel, baptized 16 November 1833, age 25 years, daughter of Pierre-Ferdinand Wenzel and Agathe Letendre, C. E. Poire. (page 117)

Wenzel, Alexandre

B-570, Alexandre Wenzel, baptized 6 April 1833, age 27 years, son of Ferdinand Wenzel and Magdeleine Montagnaise, Godfather: Louis L'Arrivee, G. A. Belcourt priest. (page 97)

Whitford, Genevieve

B-588, Genevieve Wetford, baptized [between 17-22 May] 1833, born 12 May 1833, of the legitimate marriage of Francois Wetford and Marie [Gladu], Godfather: Francois Morin, Godmother: Genevieve .., F. Boucher priest. (page 101)

Wilkey, Augustin

B-589, Augustin Wilkey, baptized 15 November 1829, age about 5 __, of the legitimate marriage of Jean-Baptiste Wilkey and Amable Azure, Godfather: Martin Jerome, Godmother: Miss Marguerite Nolin (signed), Frs. Boucher priest. (page 34)

Wilky, Catherine

B-895, Catherine Wilky, baptized 25 November 1834, born yesterday of the legitimate marriage of Jean Baptiste Wilky and Amable [Azur], Godfather: Jean Baptiste Davis, Godmother: [Ma]delaine Azur, J. N. Ev de Juliopolis. (page 156)

Yankoski, Joseph

S__, Joseph Yankoski, buired [between 9 and 18 May 1834], died yesterday, age 5 years, legitimate son of [Antoine] Yankoski and Josephte Roi, in the presence of Isidore .. and Louis Bousquet, C. E. Poire priest. (page 128)

Yauski, Josephte

B-584, Josephte Yauski, baptized 15 May 1833, born of the legitimate marriage of Antoine Yauski and Josephte Roi, Godfather: William Shaw (signed), Godmother: Magdeleine Isaac, C. E. Poire priest. (page 100)

Yinini, Marguerite

S-43, Marguerite Yinini, buried 16 May 1833, daughter of Yinini Sauteux and Ok.... Sauteuse, in the presence of William Shaw (signed) and .., C. E. Poire priest. (page 100)

Zace, Angelique

B-444, Angelique Zace, baptized 10 June 1832, born 1 June 1832, of Louise de Gonzaque Zace and Angelique Parisien, Godfather: Andre Carriere, Godmother: Genevieve Lafrance [?], G. A. Belcourt priest. (page 67)

Zace, Genevieve

B-792, Genevieve Zace, baptized 1 June 1834, born yesterday of the legitimate marriage of Gonzague Zace and Angelique Parisien, Godfather: Louis Delorme, Godmother: Genevieve Larence, J. B. Thibault priest. (page 129)

Zace, Gonzague and Angelique Parisien

M-106, Gonzague Zace, adult son of the late Andre Zace and the deceased Marie Sans Souses of the Berthier district, married 28 May 1833, Angelique Parisien, adult daughter of Jean Baptiste Parisien and Louise Farier, in the presence of Joseph Parenteau and Joseph Lafournaise, F. Boucher priest. (page 104)

www.ingramcontent.com/pod-product-compliance
Lightning Source LLC
Chambersburg PA
CBHW081841280526
45789CB00007B/2532